'Your perf[...] [...] [...] career
le[...]. savour it like good wine.'
—R. Gopalakrishnan, director, Tata Sons Ltd

'There are many books with mantras and career tips for navigating the corporate world, but for me what works best in Partha's book is how his ideas subtly enter the subconscious. And this, in my experience, is invaluable—not what is learnt but what is felt and internalized.'
—Prasoon Joshi, poet and chairman and CEO, McCann Worldgroup India

'Partha succinctly converts tricky situations in the corporate world into accessible stories that will hugely benefit new entrants.'
—Rajiv Memani, CEO, Ernst & Young India

'Dexterously woven and artfully subtle, Basu offers a simple yet comprehensive recipe for winning:
build trust, build a reputation, build a network, then break all the rules!'
—Nihal Kaviratne CBE, vice chairman, Indian Cancer Society

'Winning in the corporate world calls for passion, intuition, teamwork, innovation and lateral thinking. Partha offers radical ideas to the ambitious.'
—T.V. Mohandas Pai, chairman, Manipal Global Education Services Pvt. Ltd

PORTFOLIO

MAKE IT OR BREAK IT

Partha Sarathi Basu has worked in leadership positions for many successful corporates like AkzoNobel, Whirlpool India, Spice Jet Ltd, Coca-Cola India, Tata Group and IFB Group. He also appears as a guest lecturer in many management institutes and contributes management-related articles to magazines. His books include *Why Not . . .! Racing Ahead with Mentors* and the novel *With or without You*. Partha lives in Gurgaon and loves to read, travel, watch movies, play sports and observe human behaviour. Readers can find out more about him at www.parthasarathibasu.com.

MAKE IT
OR
BREAK IT

MANTRAS FOR A SUCCESSFUL CAREER

PARTHA SARATHI BASU

PORTFOLIO
PENGUIN

PORTFOLIO
Published by the Penguin Group
Penguin Books India Pvt. Ltd, 11 Community Centre, Panchsheel Park,
New Delhi 110 017, India
Penguin Group (USA) Inc., 375 Hudson Street, New York, New York 10014, USA
Penguin Group (Canada), 90 Eglinton Avenue East, Suite 700, Toronto, Ontario,
M4P 2Y3, Canada (a division of Pearson Penguin Canada Inc.)
Penguin Books Ltd, 80 Strand, London WC2R 0RL, England
Penguin Ireland, 25 St Stephen's Green, Dublin 2, Ireland (a division of Penguin
Books Ltd)
Penguin Group (Australia), 707 Collins Street, Melbourne, Victoria 3008, Australia
(a division of Pearson Australia Group Pty Ltd)
Penguin Group (NZ), 67 Apollo Drive, Rosedale, Auckland 0632, New Zealand
(a division of Pearson New Zealand Ltd)
Penguin Group (South Africa) (Pty) Ltd, 24 Sturdee Avenue, Rosebank, Johannesburg
2196, South Africa

Penguin Books Ltd, Registered Offices: 80 Strand, London WC2R 0RL, England

First published in Portfolio by Penguin Books India 2012

Copyright © Partha Sarathi Basu 2012

ISBN 9780143418665

Typeset in Garamond by R. Ajith Kumar, New Delhi
Printed at Replika Press Pvt. Ltd, Sonepat

ALWAYS LEARNING   **PEARSON**

To Ma and Baba,
for their most valuable guidance in my initial years

CONTENTS

PREFACE

Transitionary phases in any realm can be sensitive and complex. More so, the transitions that have a lasting impact on the vocational progress of an individual. *Make It or Break It: Mantras for a Successful Career* handles this very sensitive issue in a practical manner and, most importantly, sans pontification.

The narrative is simple, lucid and replete with anecdotes which greatly ease comprehending the complexities of the issue. The basic construct of the book is such that it deals with the entire cycle of getting in the corporate world, surviving it and emerging triumphant out of it. No aspect, which can have an impact on the career of a young professional and which he should watch out for, has been left unattended by Mr Basu in this book. In fact, I can safely state that the book is a microcosm of the collective wisdom required to transit smoothly from campus to corporate.

The easy prose and the anecdotes, which are easy to relate to, prefacing each 'mantra' not only make an interesting read but also put it in proper perspective.

It's a *Lonely Planet* for aspiring professionals fresh out of campus—a must-read for every young professional!

Renu Karnad
MD, HDFC Ltd
and Businesswoman of the Year 2010

PROLOGUE

I looked at my watch; I still had an hour to go. I guessed I could reach the auditorium. I quickly checked my bag; the brown envelope was inside. I picked up the car keys and rushed towards the parking lot. As I exited the underground parking, I realized I had to drive really fast. I needed to catch up with him, hand the treasure over to him. I couldn't miss this opportunity.

I reached my destination and crossed the auditorium gate. I found the old man sitting on the dais. He looked the same, just as I had last met him many years ago, except that his biological age had gone up by several years and his hair had greyed a little. To me, though, he looked as young, as energetic, as learned as ever.

The auditorium was nearly full; I could barely manage a chair at the back. As usual, his sharp eyes didn't miss me. He slowly raised his hand and waved at me. I knew he hadn't changed a bit. I smiled, waving back. I could sense that I was still in awe of him.

He got up to speak, and said, 'Thanks everyone for this evening. I am honoured. For many years, I have spoken at many forums, attended many seminars. I never thought that one day I would decide to hang up my boots. Over the last many years, I ran from one place to another, from one position to another. I never felt tired. I enjoyed every bit of it. But then, one day, I sat down with myself and spoke to my Chief, my inner self. I asked him: "What's next?"

'My Chief replied: "Enough of running. It's time to give back to the world." I agreed with my Chief, but wondered how. We spoke again and decided that I should now dedicate the rest of my life to guiding young people, handholding them. I must share my experiences, my learning. My Chief said that it would be my payback to this corporate jungle. Today, I feel extremely proud as I look around at this esteemed audience. I can feel the buzz. I feel privileged that my country has so much talent waiting in the wings. Thanks for being here and making my day special.'

He paused for a moment and added, 'I must share one more thing. I feel particularly happy to see one face here. I never expected him to be here. We have a very successful young man sitting in the audience. I have not met him for many years, but today I know that we have not forgotten each other. We still have enough stories to share.'

He pointed his finger at me. I stood up and he called me on to the stage. A bit embarrassed, I walked up, the brown envelope held tight in my hand. I touched his feet. He blessed me as I said, 'Thank you sir.'

He smiled, took my hands in his, and turned to the audience, saying, 'This is the man who first gave me the courage to teach. I still remember the day I first saw him. He had barely entered the corporate world but was the first to challenge my corporate wisdom. Imagine—he was then a management trainee and I the group CEO!' He paused, inhaled deeply and said, 'He did not agree with what I was preaching then. I liked that. I took on the challenge to convince him. It took me a few weeks before I saw a smile on his face.'

I stood next to him, and Mr Chatterjee carried on, 'I am not sure how much justice I did that day, but today I feel proud to see that he has reached where many successful people dream of reaching. He is the CEO of a very large corporation. I am sure most of you know him well.' He smiled and looked at me.

I said, 'Thank you, sir. Those few weeks made me what I am today.'

Then, I handed over the packet to him and said, 'This is for you, sir.'

He looked a bit surprised and asked, 'What's inside?'

'A gift from a young man to another young man, who will live in his heart forever.'

He smiled and opened the envelope. It was a manuscript, dedicated to him.

I said, 'I have captured all that you told me years ago, in those few sessions.'

He read the first line: 'Once upon a time . . .'

Tears rolled down his eyes. He hugged me, and patted me on my shoulder. It was the greatest gift I received in my life.

Many years ago

It had barely been a few months since I had entered the corporate world.

One evening, Mr Vivek Chatterjee, our group CEO, was addressing the management trainees in his office. It was part of our regular induction sessions. Earlier, in our few interactions with him, we had understood that he liked to spend extra time with young minds. He liked to share his insights of the practical world. He was different, a great speaker, no airs about being the CEO. We all liked his way of teaching since it was a respite from all the boring lectures we had to hear. We looked forward to his sessions.

He believed that interacting with us helped him understand our generation better. He would say, 'I feel much younger when I meet the youth. I learn so much. I get a new perspective on today's world.'

The feeling that at least someone cared for our opinion was quite encouraging for us.

That day, he was discussing the transition from a 'college dude to a corporate honcho'. After a brief introduction, he said, 'These early days are like a roller-coaster ride. You may not like them but, later in life as you think back, you will treasure every one of these memories. You will realize that you wouldn't have achieved much without these years. In these formative days, every moment is an experience. You need to go through the grind. It is a necessary evil. Good or bad does not matter.

'Corporate life can be a fun-filled journey, it depends on

you. In any case, it will be different, very different from the journey you have had so far. They call it a rat race—I call it a fat race. The better you run, the fatter your salary package, the higher your designation.'

We all laughed. I liked the concept of 'fat race'.

Mr Chatterjee continued, 'Let's put some facts on the table. We all have dreams in life. At every step, we may define a new dream or reaffirm one we have seen for ourselves. I am not here to define your dream. It is your dream. Everyone has his own dream. We all decide to become "something", "someone different", perhaps, or "someone important". That is ours to decide. Every dream is unique. It is meant to be.

'Thus we study, learn, score high marks and finally land up at a job interview. We do well there and grab the job we think is right for us . . . That's the way most of us start our corporate lives, to pursue the dream that we had dreamt for ourselves. Thus everything, I repeat *everything*, we do is important from the day we accept the job offer since the corporate world is the place where we have chosen to chase our dream.

'We must recognize that our journey in the corporate world will be completely different from the lives we have led so far. It's a practical world, and all those theories and problems that you have solved through late nights may be of little use. You will feel distressed, you will feel lost. You will ask yourself, "What the hell am I doing here?" You will fret: "Why did I study so much, when I do not use my education in the real sense?" But those moments are important too. Those moments of despair, that sense of losing direction will make you a true professional one day.

'I really do believe that the first few years are the most important years of your corporate voyage. These few years will make you fit enough to run every other day in this corporate fat race. Your first few years can decide if you are making or breaking your career . . .'

He had hardly finished but I responded, 'If you allow me to argue, I do not agree with you at all. I think if you have the zeal to succeed, you are bound to go ahead. I know many people who failed in their early lives but excelled afterwards in their careers.'

Mr Chatterjee smiled. I could sense that he had guessed that I did not believe in what he preached. He said, 'I think you got me wrong, young man. I never said you can't be successful after an early failure. What I meant was that you must ensure that in first few years you shape yourself well for a successful career. I said these are probably the most important years of your career.'

'I still do not agree with you, sir. It does not matter where I start. What matters is where I finish,' I replied.

'True, but it matters how you start as well. Do you agree with me?'

'Not really, sir.'

Mr Chatterjee looked thoughtful and said, 'Well, then we have a problem in hand. What do we do?'

I said bluntly, 'I don't think you need to be bothered about it. It is not necessary that I agree with all your views. I am listening to you, sir. Let me absorb what I like to absorb.'

'Fair enough! I'm happy that you are expressing your thoughts fearlessly. In today's world, I find very few people doing that. It will remain my duty to explain to you what I mean. At the end, we may not agree, but I will still try.'

I nodded. Mr Chatterjee said, solicitously, 'We have enough examples in this world to prove you right, but they are limited—only a few out of the large population of this world. And because there are some people who succeeded after early failures, it does not follow that everyone must fail before succeeding! I feel strongly that we should not take a few proven examples and generalize a theory. Early failure or early success are immaterial—what I meant was how you should spend the first few years that will shape you for a better tomorrow. Those years are important. They are critical.'

The office room burst into murmurs. I could sense his eyes fixed on me. I was uncomfortable. I could sense that he was trying to gauge my reaction. I felt miserable. I'd challenged the CEO within weeks of joining the company. Yet I managed to look confident, since I believed in what I had said. I kept quiet, waiting for Mr Chatterjee to speak again.

He said, 'Thank you for accepting my logic. Let us move ahead . . .'

Now, I stood up and said, 'Sir, you will be mistaken if you think that I have accepted your logic. I have not. But I would urge you to go ahead and finish your lecture. I would not want you and others to suffer because of my stupid beliefs.' My retort was, yet again, caustic.

He was undeterred; he was calm and composed. He

smiled as I said, 'I promise to keep quiet. My conscience does not allow me to argue with my senior in an open forum over a point about which I will never get convinced.'

He said, 'I like your conviction, I like your challenge. So should I accept the challenge to convince you?'

I replied softly, 'I won't mind, sir, but then you need to tell me all I need to do in my first few years to sail through the rest of my life.' He could barely hear me.

'I can't promise to tell you everything, since it is a process of discovery. I will, however, share with you what I learnt during *my* corporate journey. I am sure you will pick up the rest during yours.'

I nodded and he said, 'I think this will be fun. Who knows? Perhaps I will get some more important lessons for life out of these discussions!'

He then scanned the gathering and asked, 'I need a few sessions to speak my mind. I do not know how I will find the time, but I will. Let us meet every Saturday at my club. We will spend the day together. This means you will have to make time for me during your weekends. Is that acceptable?'

All the young management trainees present in the room were thrilled. They could not believe that Mr Chatterjee would be making time for them during his weekends.

Mr Chatterjee added, 'In my childhood, every evening before I went to bed, my mother told me new tales. I loved all of them. I always wondered how she had such a vast repertory. Much later I realized that she used to draw those stories from her real life. They were so real and so close to life that I still remember them. My mother has passed that habit on to me. I too love to tell stories. In the time that we spend together, I will narrate some stories from the corporate world.

'No boring lectures, I promise! Interestingly, I find common threads between my stories and those my mother narrated. My mother's stories always started with "once upon a time". They had a young man or woman—the protagonist—and a king or a queen. Most of them ended happily.'

We laughed. He then declared, 'Similarly, all my stories will start with "once upon a time". See you all at my club, this Saturday at 10 a.m.'

Mr Chatterjee left the room. We all wondered what awaited us on Saturday.

SECTION 1
GETTING INTO THE JUNGLE

It was a sunny winter morning. All of us reached the club much before the scheduled time. I felt excited, but I did not speak much. I simply waited for the big man to arrive.

Mr Chatterjee arrived right on time. Wearing blue jeans, a red T-shirt and sunglasses, he looked cheerful and ready to take on the day. We sat by the pool and he began, 'Good morning folks. Call me Vivek, and treat me as your friend. Give me comfort, open up to me, make me feel like a part of your group. That is the only way we can enjoy this journey together. And please remember that this is *your* day—I am just a storyteller.'

We settled down. Mr Chatterjee said, 'The corporate world is a jungle. It is ruthless. The theory of survival of the fittest is most applicable here. Hence, to pursue your dream, you need to learn the trick of survival quickly.

'I will divide these sessions of ours into four phases. We will talk about: (1) how you should get into the jungle, then (2) how to walk through the jungle, after that (3) how to survive in the jungle and finally (4) how to emerge as winners from this jungle.

'But your life will not end after these first few years; you need to keep walking to fulfil your dream. What I will share in these few days will probably help you along in your journey. After I narrate each story, I will summarize my views. You have every right to tell me that you do not agree with me. I hope that's okay with you.'

We agreed.

'As we start our journey today, we need to begin from the premise that we have made a lasting commitment to the corporate world. It is a new life for us, most of which is unknown. We will uncover the mystery as we go along. Thus, the first step is to accept that we may need to change to adapt to this new world. Here you may have a basic question—if you have led a successful life till now, why do you need to change? Well, you need to change because you are an alien in this world. Your past learning may lead you to behave in a certain way, which may not be the behaviour the corporate jungle expects. The rules of this jungle are different. The sooner you accept this reality, the quicker you learn and adapt, the faster you will fulfil your dreams.'

He paused for a moment and asked, 'So shall we start?'

Accept the transition

When our first parents were driven out of paradise, Adam is believed to have remarked to Eve: 'My dear, we live in the age of transition.'—Dean Inge

Once upon a time, there was a young lady who joined a large knowledge process outsourcing enterprise, as a trainee in their planning vertical. Her induction coincided with the annual planning cycle—it was the time of the year when the team finalized its profit plan for the next year. It was a busy period and the planning team worked late each day, even through the weekends.

One Friday, the King, the head of the planning department, called an urgent meeting around 6 p.m. When the team members gathered in the conference room, the King said, 'I have some news for you guys. Our deadline has been squeezed further. The boss wants to review the first-cut data on Monday morning.'

The team members looked at each other, waiting for the King to finish. The King continued, 'I am a bit nervous now. We have a mammoth task at hand.'

The team listened in silence. The King finally declared, 'Let us meet tomorrow at 9 a.m. I guess we need to work this Sunday as well. Please update me on the progress status at 10 p.m. tonight. I will be staying back in the office till I get the update.'

The team agreed. As everyone got up to go back to work, the young lady said to the King, 'But, your highness, today is Friday.'

The King frowned at her and asked sardonically, 'So?' The young lady started to reply but he intervened, 'It is just 7 p.m. We have a long day ahead.'

'But, your highness, I have a party to attend,' exclaimed the young lady.

The rest of the team sniggered as the King said, 'That's interesting. But, young lady, we also have a task to deliver by Monday.'

Feeling too confident, the young lady said, 'But, your highness, what if we deliver the project a day later?'

The King laughed and replied, 'We have a deadline to meet. The boss wants the results early. I have fixed the meeting at 10 a.m. on Monday. That's it. We live to deliver results on time. If our customers are not happy, we cannot justify our salaries.'

No one spoke. Now the young girl said, 'I'm new to this job and still learning. I don't think, if I leave early, my contribution will be missed.'

The others could feel that the King was being pushed to the limits of his patience. However, to their surprise, he kept his cool and said, 'You aren't alone any more, young lady. You are part of this team. I suggest that you be here with the team. They would love your presence and you may learn faster.'

'But, your highness,' fumbled the young lady, 'I have friends waiting downstairs. I have a party to attend. Immediately after the party, we are meant to leave for a weekend trip.'

Disgusted, the King raised his voice a bit and said, 'Now listen to me carefully. I don't care that you have friends waiting. I have advised you to be here. It will be good for you. Hope you get my message.' He left the room. The team followed.

The young lady sat quietly in the conference room for a while, thinking. She could not find any logic of her staying back. In her mind, she was convinced that she couldn't add any value to the process. Why waste the weekend, she thought. She left the office in some time for the party, followed by the weekend trip. When she returned to the office on Monday morning, the King called her to his room and had a long discussion with her. And they never lived happily ever after.

We may need a complete mental makeover as we start our corporate journey. The first thing to do is to accept that we are not ready to face the new life. We need to remind ourselves every moment that life will be different—indeed, life is different already—and that we need to change our minds to suit this world and its lifestyle.

Most of you may think that you are ready, but you may not really be, since college may not have taught you several things that you would need every day as you walk through this jungle. Pause for a moment, think of the classroom you were in, sitting next to a friend you chose. Think of the day you dropped everything else, perhaps an appointment with your fiancé or a date with your heart-throb, and rushed to listen to your favourite teacher's lecture. Think of the day you bunked class to watch the latest blockbuster movie, first-day-first-show. Think of the day you scored a century in a cricket match at the college ground, feel again the cheering all around you. Think of that free kick that crossed the goalpost in the football final against your rival college. Or just think of the day you were sick in your hostel room, and all your friends gathered around you just to be with you . . . Those were the days, right?

Time went by and you became part of the seniormost class of your college. Then came the examinations—you did well, but that was the end of your college life. Your education has brought you here. You now have the job you always wanted. This is the job that will help you chase your dreams. Don't worry, though—your journey in the corporate world will also be fun, but this has to be a different fun from your college life.

In these sessions, we will talk about the probable changes we need to bring in ourselves. To start with, we need to understand that unlike college life, the life in the corporate world involves less of 'I' and more of 'we'. Till now, it was your education, your degree, your achievements. But now you are not alone—you work for a company, a team.

We are no longer working towards our own goals, but towards a team's goal, for a team's success. As we have seen in this story, the young lady failed to understand the need of her presence with the team during the weekend. She failed to understand that this world was different and that she needed to adjust to her new life.

So, welcome to the real world, my friends. It is a world full of dreams and opportunities, but if you don't adjust to it well, it can easily lead you down the path of despair. It's easy to lose in this corporate jungle, but when we win, it will be a victory to cherish forever. When you decide to accept the transition and change yourself to suit this new world, your goal will be nearer with every passing day.

Manage your own expectations

Not knowing when the dawn will come, I open every door.
—Emily Dickinson

Once upon a time, a young man joined an automotive manufacturer after four years of studying engineering at a premier college. He was intelligent and meritorious. His dream was to design a car that would take the global roads by surprise. When he got the opportunity to work for one of the largest automotive manufacturers in the country, he was ecstatic that his dream would be fulfilled.

The young man joined his office, ready to give his best and prove his worth to the organization. He opted for a position in their global design cell under a very senior officer, the King of the design department.

Some months passed by. The young man completed his orientation and training. He was then formally absorbed into the global design cell. The King assigned him a job in the record department—to keep track of all the drawings. The King advised him, 'I want you to understand how the designs are tracked and when they are used. It will help you in the future.'

Within months, the young man started feeling unhappy at his post. He felt that it did not suit his education or calibre—after all, he was not designing cars. It bothered him that his talent was not being utilized properly. He decided to meet the King for a discussion.

The King heard him, and agreed to offer him another position. This time, the young man's job was to keep track of all project expenditures. The King told him, 'Keeping track of expenditure will help you understand the importance of money. I want you to learn this.'

In a few months, the young man was frustrated again. This time, he discussed the matter with his friends. They too were convinced that he was being fooled by the King. They advised him to leave the job without wasting any more time. He liked their advice, since it was exactly what he believed—that he deserved better-quality work. Keeping track of expenditure was way below his intellectual level. He met the King again, this time to challenge him.

He said, 'Your highness, I think you are not utilizing my talent. I can do a lot more. At university, I scored record marks in industrial design. I was the best in my batch. I have not joined work to keep track of how much is being spent and how. That is the job of a junior officer. This is such a waste of my potential!'

The King smiled and asked, 'What has gone wrong in the last few weeks?'

'Everything, your highness. I am wasting my talent. I will be lagging behind in my career if I continue with what I am doing today.'

The King said, 'Young man, I appreciate your sense of urgency and the fire in you to prove your worth. I also know that you were the best in your batch, which is why I hired you. But you must appreciate that you are just an uncut diamond, which has negligible value. My job is to give you lustre. What I am doing now is giving your raw talent and energy the facets and the shape, so that in the future, you can be a business leader and a great designer. What you are doing today may not be fancy by your standards, but this knowledge will empower you to understand the business. There's no point in designing a great car if you do not know how it affects the business. We respect talented people like you and know how to train them as future leaders. I urge you to follow my guidelines; you will not regret it later.'

The young man did not immediately agree with what the King said. He continued to mull over leaving the job to pursue his interest in design. The King sensed his desperation, and, over the next few weeks, he spent a lot more time talking to the young man and explaining the rationale behind his actions. It was a trying time for the King, but, after many counselling sessions, he was able to convince the young man that he was on the right path and not losing out. And they lived happily ever after.

The young man in this story was lucky to get a King like that, who spent many hours convincing him. You may not always be so fortunate.

It is true that most people who have reached the top started at the baseline. They dirtied their hands to get a holistic picture of the business. This training is vital. Most successful companies ensure that their trainees are exposed to different facets of the business before being absorbed.

Let us learn the basics, do all the so-called dirty jobs that we are not supposed to do. It is our chance to learn what happens in different parts of the organization, at the ground level. We may not get this opportunity later in our career, once we get busy with core activities.

Every experience is important—it comes in handy at some point or the other in our career. We must never feel that we are doing a job that is beneath our potential. Such considerations are all in our minds. All jobs are important. It is imperative to perform those so-called mundane, not-so-intellectual jobs.

The young man, having graduated from one of the best engineering colleges, didn't want to wait. He was in a hurry. He believed in his ability and that made him restless. His urge to design his dream car egged him on.

But what the King told him was right. He knew that once the young man reached the corporate level, the overall knowledge would give him the authority to relate to the business. The King knew the importance of these basic jobs; he knew how to shape raw talent. He knew that if he were not guided, the young man would remain a great designer but fail to become a business manager in the long run.

So, if you are asked to do some photocopying in the first few years of your career, try not to feel bad about it. Who knows, you might become the CEO of Xerox Corporation one day!

Unlearn and relearn

The illiterate of the 21st century will not be those who cannot read and write, but those who cannot learn, unlearn and relearn.—Alvin Toffler

Once upon a time, there was a King who was the human resources head of a company. One morning, he was addressing a group of young people who had just joined the company. The King said, 'Welcome aboard. Please tighten your seatbelts, for we are about to take off. Our destination today is our dream space—this flight can take us anywhere we wish to reach. We can decide to reach the absolute top or the rock bottom. Looking at you, it seems to me that none of you are here to fail in your careers, so I would assume that you all want to reach the peak. But, as we start our journey today, we need to change our thought processes. We need to open our minds. Please remind yourself that your education is not complete, even though you have earned your degrees. Treat yourselves as toddlers who have just started schooling, prepare yourselves to shed some baggage of past education, and choose to unlearn a few things and relearn many.'

The group laughed in unison. The King said, 'I am happy that you all laughed. This shows that you are no different from the normal young professionals that I meet every year. Of course, you do not believe in what I just said.'

The King's sarcastic comment stung the group of young people into silence. He continued, 'Now let us understand what I meant. There are many rules in this corporate world, the first is to unlearn and relearn. We all have decided to fly to the zenith, and that is the destination for all of us. As the pilot of this flight, I will take off only when we all agree that we are ready to unlearn and relearn.'

A pensive young man stood up and asked, 'Your highness, do you suggest that we need to forget our hard-earned education? Do you imply that whatever we learnt in the last several years is not required any longer?'

'Not really, but the corporate world is a practical

world. What matters here is the real application of your education. As you walk through this corporate jungle, you will realize that the jungle itself will teach you what you need to know. You must keep your mind open and keep learning. Learn from the whisper, learn from the noise, learn from the quietness. Every moment, treat yourself as a student hungry for more. To do that, you must empty your minds and make space for this fresh knowledge.'

The King looked at the crowd and said, 'If you agree with me to start afresh, we can fly. Shall we?'

The young men and women agreed . . . And they lived happily ever after.

We accept any new job, whether fresh out of college or otherwise, with a mindset. Our past experience or education plays on our mind. We must always use our experience and knowledge, but then, we need to be careful about the application since every company is different and so is every job. Carrying too much 'legacy' will hamper our performance. It will affect our new learning opportunities and hence the progress of our career.

Unlearning allows us to keep our minds open to new ideas, and also shed some of our beliefs and theoretical knowledge, in order to suit the corporate world. All the theories that we learn at college are important, but their applications differ from industry to industry. Having an open mind will help us use our knowledge optimally.

Let us look at the last few decades. People unlearnt using a typewriter to get used to a computer. The fixed phone was replaced by mobile technology. We seldom post physical letters, but use e-mail all the time. Instead of waiting at the bank for hours to withdraw money, we use ATMs. Society has changed, as has the corporate world. And they will change further . . .

Through all these examples, we must recognize one thing—as a society, we have unlearnt a few things and relearnt several. It was not easy for any of us yet we did, as that was needed to suit ourselves to 'today'. It is a painfully slow process and requires an internal change management deep inside us.

But let us not forget that all knowledge and experience is useful. We should store and use it when we need it. Who knows, one day, we may need to relearn what we have just unlearnt!

Mr Chatterjee paused for a while to look around. I sensed a smile of satisfaction on his face. I too looked around, noticed a few mesmerized faces. Everybody looked engrossed in what they were hearing. No one spoke; the silence was unbelievable. I sensed a dual feeling of satisfaction and disbelief. Mr Chatterjee broke the silence, 'Wake up guys! Let's take a break to move around and absorb what we have discussed. The next step will be to know our surroundings.'

Understand the culture

You can't cross the sea merely by standing and staring at the water. —Rabindranath Tagore

Once upon a time, there was a young man who worked for a British multinational in London. This young man had a good track record—he had done well in the first few years at his earlier job. He had joined his current company about a year ago, after having worked with its American competitor. This company had great HR practices. One of the practices was to identify talented people and put them on differential career paths. At an annual meeting, every possible candidate for this role was discussed at great length. All members of the leadership team had to agree on a candidate before the name was included in the final list. If anyone disagreed, either that member had to be convinced—the onus being on the supervisor of the individual being discussed—or the candidature would not appear in the final list.

It was an important process for every individual as well as for the company since these candidates were treated differently, their careers monitored separately, and they were on differential perks and salaries. Every senior leader needed to take ownership of these associates.

That year, after this young man's case was argued to the satisfaction of most leaders by his superior, the King said, 'Gentlemen, I am not sure that we are doing justice to other talents by putting this young man ahead of the many good associates that we have. I believe it is too early for him to be recognized as our top talent. In fact, he needs to adapt himself to our rich culture before he is even discussed in this august forum.'

When the HR head asked for the reason, the King explained, 'Well, he does not even respect people. He calls everybody, even seniors, by their first names. The other day, in a meeting, he called me by my first name, knowing full well that I am a leadership team member. I am sure you will appreciate that this is against the etiquette and culture of our organization.'

The group agreed and advised the young man's supervisor to counsel him so that he could adapt to the culture and figure in the top talent list the next year. The supervisor had a discussion with the young man, who understood the problem and agreed to follow the organizational culture. And they lived happily ever after.

Every company is different. It has its own culture. It evolves over time. The associates respect its traditions and values; they take pride in them. It is important for every new individual to adapt to the company's culture. Each organization also has its dos and don'ts. Some practices are acceptable, some are not. Often, there are unwritten rules, which need to be remembered and followed all the time. The problem is that there may not be a formal process to guide you through these rules. You are expected to understand them intuitively. The onus of adapting to the new culture lies on you. Going an extra step to find out and follow the unwritten rules in a new culture will smoothen your journey.

This young man's example is not an uncommon one. When he moved in to this organization, he did not recognize the change. For him, calling everybody by his or her first name was natural, as that is what he had learnt in his earlier organization. He was not wrong, but in his new company, he was expected to behave differently. It had different expectations from an individual. The practices acceptable in his earlier company were not appreciated here. So he had to change.

The King genuinely believed in what he said—he was quite shocked when this young man had called him by his first name. He expected to be addressed as either Sir or Mr. It was natural to him, an unwritten rule in his mind. Thus he objected. Though this young man was brilliant at his work, he failed to meet the expectations of his senior colleagues by not adapting to the culture of the company.

Know your seniors

I've always found that the speed of the boss is the speed of the team.—Lee Iacocca

Once upon a time, there was a young man who joined an Indian MNC as a corporate planner. This young man moved into the company as a lateral hire; he had two years of work experience from an earlier job, which he had quit to earn his MBA degree.

In the company, getting into the planning role was never easy, since the job required regular interaction with the senior management. The planning department thus always looked for the best talent. The young man showed immense maturity and acumen during the interview process, and thus bagged the job.

This young man's immediate boss was a lady who headed corporate planning. She was also the blue-eyed girl of the King, the company's CFO. Obviously, she was good at her work.

The young man watched his boss's work style closely. He found that she spent disproportionate lengths of time working with the King, and was never there to guide him, never available for any discussion. This frustrated the young man, but he never dared to ask her for more time. From his sources in the office he learnt that the King trusted her a lot and took actions based on the feedback that she, his boss, provided him. In fact, the King's boss, the company's MD, also depended on this lady's business acumen. Very often, people would notice the MD himself walking into her office to spend time with her.

The King had another habit. If the lady was unavailable, the King would walk up to this young man's desk and ask for information. This gesture of the King always made him nervous since he knew that his boss, the lady, did not like him interacting directly with the King.

During his first appraisal, the young man realized that his boss was not too happy with his performance. He disagreed with her assessment of him because, to his mind, he was probably giving more to the company than was expected of him. He always worked late hours and arrived at valued analyses, which his boss often shared with the King or the MD. But when he asked her how he might improve his performance, she could not give him any concrete message.

The young man kept the feedback in mind and tried to work even better. One day, just after the King left the young man's desk, his boss called him and said, 'I know that you had a few years of experience before you pursued your MBA but those don't mean anything to me. To me, you are almost a fresher; you lack maturity. I do not want you to give any information to any senior people without consulting me.'

Her tone was polite but her voice was firm and intimidating. She added, 'The management makes decisions based on what we say, so we need to be careful. Please run all details by me before you hand them over to the King.'

The young man realized the real issue. His performance was hardly under question—the concern was different. The lady did not like his direct interactions with the King. She was insecure about sharing the space of privilege with him. She enjoyed her proximity with the top management.

The young man was in a predicament. He wondered how he could manage such a situation. By not sharing any details, he would be at a greater risk since the King might feel that he was not performing well enough. On the other hand, he couldn't tell the King that his boss had ordered him not to share any information without informing her. That would go against him as well.

He finally came up with smarter ways. At times, he kept the lady informed about the information he passed on to the King. At other times, he asked for some extra time so he could rush to the lady and show her the document he was planning to hand over to the King. His process worked, and he lived happily ever after.

These situations aren't new. We all face such dilemmas in our day-to-day corporate lives. Every individual is different; no two persons are the same and neither are two bosses. Thus, there is no unique formula to deal with your boss. The only way out is to know him or her well.

You have a character of your own—you are unique. Similarly, your boss has a character of his own and he is unique too. Never expect your boss to be like you. Some will be easy to talk to; some will love to keep distance. Some will call you home and interact with your family; some will not take the relationship beyond office hours. Some will confide in you; some will keep things under wraps, away from you. The list can go on and on.

Based on the personality, the style of functioning can also be different. Some will like you to walk in and keep them informed of all developments; others will like you to share information only on a need basis. Some like a call; others prefer e-mail. Some allow you to discuss an issue any time you wish; others like to get an update at a formal meeting. Some prefer you to take the lead in meetings where they are also present; others like you to remain passive, while they do all the talking. Some like a text message; others hate it.

No style is right, no style wrong. Style is pretty individualistic and gets formed over years, based on upbringing, social environment and experience, among other factors. What is important is for you to know which style your boss prefers. If you try and adapt to his style of interaction, it will ease your interaction. Do not get me wrong. This does not mean that you are changing your basic style or doing something to massage your boss's ego. No way. You are just helping yourself by ensuring that your working styles are synchronized. That's all.

Look at what this young man did. He learnt the hard way, since initially he did not make an effort to find out what his boss liked or disliked. But then, his boss spoke to him directly and indicated the need for change. He was lucky to get an opportunity to rectify the damage quickly. You may not be so lucky.

Know your peers

In peers, let us find a friend.—Popular saying

Once upon a time, there was a young lady who joined the corporate world. The King, the head of the HR department, habitually kept track of all newcomers till they were comfortable in the new environment and had settled down in their jobs. He was very particular about watching them closely and worked as a mentor to them during their initial days. He had some people to help him and, this time, he assigned the job to a young man to ensure that this young lady settled down completely in the new environment.

The company had a large office, spread over nine floors. One day, the young man reported an unusual habit of this young lady to the King. He had observed that she used the stairs instead of the elevator. The King was happy—he thought she was a fitness freak! But the young man was not comfortable and reported the matter again when he got suspicious. He also found that every time the young lady emerged from a meeting, she would stand at the corner of the stairs, noting down something in her diary. He found that unnatural.

The King wanted to ignore the matter but, with the young man's growing uneasiness, he too got apprehensive. He decided to keep track of the young lady himself. When he too noticed her unusual habits over a few days, he decided to confront the lady directly.

What he found out was interesting. The young lady said that since she was undergoing an induction programme she was introduced to many new colleagues every day. In such a large organization, she met too many new faces and it was extremely difficult for her to remember their personal details. Thus, as soon as she was out of a meeting, she would walk towards the stairs and note down their details in her notebook. She wanted to remember everyone's 'little detail' which was beyond their normal job description, things that were personal in nature and were shared during her interaction with them. She used the stairs, as that was the only place in the office with few people, and she could spend some time there in isolation.

She said, 'My mother taught me one thing that I will never forget. She told me that my name, my memories and my date of birth are my own—mine alone. Everything else has to be shared. I strongly believe that a little personal touch like a wish on someone's birthday can take the relationship a long way.'

The King smiled, feeling bad for doubting the young lady's intentions. And they lived happily ever after.

In the corporate world, it is vital for you to know the people around you. You are the new kid on the block, and you must take the initiative. Let us recognize the fact that life prevailed in your offices even before you joined. The urge to know the people around you well should be *yours*.

As a formal process, you will get introduced to people by your HR colleagues, but I am sure you will forget most of the names by the time you reach your cubicle. Thus, after the introductions, you should make special effort to understand who is who, what are their roles, their likes and dislikes, and probably some personal details about them. Later, it will be easier to put faces to names.

You must be open to knowing people. A 'Do Not Disturb' board across your mind will not work. Regular walks around the office and a few visits to the office canteen will help you get to know people better.

Human nature is to look for friends. It's thus natural that you will get friendly with a few colleagues quicker. This is the time when you need to be careful—you must not develop a bias against any colleague based on the opinions of your first few friends. Don't let others' opinions force preconceived notions upon you. You must meet people and know them for yourselves before forming opinions of them.

Once you start interacting with people, a time will come when you can ask them some questions unrelated to the job. Without getting too personal initially, try to find out their dates of birth, something about their family, their education, their hobbies, any special skills they may be proud of and so on. While doing this, you should also respect the culture of the country or culture you are operating in—in some places, inquiring about personal details may not be appreciated and may even land you in legal trouble for intrusion of privacy. You should hear people out with a genuinely open mind and also reciprocate by sharing personal information about yourselves. You should also be careful in disclosing the received information, which other have shared with you out of sheer trust.

Most of us, as humans, are not loners. People around us make us happy. A great relationship with our colleagues is always great for the workplace. If you have friends around, you will never feel out of place and a hard day's work will be as easy as child's play. Bad relationships at work can really impose pressure on our lives. You must be honest and accept the fact that nobody—and that includes you—is perfect. All five fingers of the hand are not the same and that is why each of them has its own utility. You need all five fingers to make a fist. It is the same in the case in the corporate world. Each individual will be different but together we will be the strength of the company.

Know your juniors

Tell me, I forget. Show me, I remember. Involve me, I understand.—Ancient Chinese proverb

Once upon a time, there was a young man who joined an organization as a trainee. The results of his final examination were yet to be declared, so his appointment was provisional. He needed to obtain a certain cut-off of marks to retain his job. However, based on his past academic record, both he and his employer were confident that he would make it.

The young man was posted to a remote factory location. The King, the company's CEO, was on a visit to that factory. A day before the King's visit, the young man came to know that he had cleared the examination with record marks, much beyond the company's requirement. The young man decided not to announce his results till the King's visit was over. After all, everybody was too busy with the visit, and he knew that the results of a trainee in such a large organization did not matter to the King.

On the day of the visit, an all-employees lunch was organized for the King to interact with his employees. The young man was present too. During the lunch, the King walked up to the young man and said, 'Congratulations, young man. I am so proud of you.'

The young man was taken by surprise. He was so sure that the King was not aware of his results that he mumbled, 'Thank you, your highness, but may I know the reason for your congratulations?'

The King smiled and said, 'You know why, young man. You came third in the university. Now work hard and succeed here the way you have succeeded in your academics.'

The King then addressed the crowd loudly, 'I seek your attention please.' He took the young man's hand in his, raised it, and said, 'We have a winner among us today. This young man has just graduated with astounding marks. Please join me in giving him a big round of applause.'

The crowd clapped and cheered, they came up one by one to congratulate the young man. The young man felt on top of the world. The King's little gesture had left him spellbound.

Many years later, after the young man had moved on to another job and the King had retired, they ran into each other at an airport. The young man then shook hands with the King and asked, 'Do you recognize me, sir?'

'Yes, of course, I do,' said the King. 'How are you?'

They spoke for some time. Before they were to part for their respective flights, the young man said, 'Sir, you may have forgotten it but I still remember our first interaction. You congratulated me for my results. I wondered how you even knew about a trainee's little achievement.'

'It may be little for others, but for you it was your biggest day. As a senior, it was my duty to know details about you and recognize you when needed. I just did my job, but I know it would have had a positive effect on your young mind.'

The young man smiled and said, 'That was probably the best recognition in my life, sir.'

The King bid goodbye. Memories of those moments lived happily ever after in the young man's mind.

Corporate life is all about people, the way we deal with them. As managers, you are responsible for your people. Hence, at first, you must make an effort to understand them well. A critical difference between a good manager and a not-so-good manager is his or her understanding of people.

Everybody joins an organization to do well; people are willing to work hard, as most of them would like to excel in their respective fields. But they are not machines. Every individual has emotions and different social views and varying needs. Everyone has different aspirations, diverse ways of looking at life. Even the motivational factors for individual associates will differ—for some, it can be mere recognition, a simple pat on the back; for others, it can be money or career advancement; and so on. Often, the needs of your people can be simple, but knowing them will give you an advantage. It is imperative to understand individuals better, or you will never figure out which lever to apply for whom.

Each company also has its own rules you need to follow, certain boundaries you need to respect. Within those boundaries, however, you can achieve results optimally when you know your people well. You should act smartly rather than blindly applying one formula for all. Knowing someone closely gives you an insight into what will work and what not, and what steps would drive the business in a positive direction with the maximum involvement from your people. And why not make the effort? After all, you will spend almost half of your day with your colleagues.

Understand corporate manners

Manners are a sensitive awareness of the feelings of others. If you have that awareness, you have good manners, no matter which fork you use.—Emily Post

Once upon a time, the King, the Chief Operating Officer of an airline, was travelling to the US in first class. The crew knew him, since he was one of the seniormost members of the management team. As the flight took off, the King called an airhostess and said, 'Hi, serve me some water.'

'Sorry, sir?' replied the young lady, looking somewhat uncomfortable.

The King was working at his computer; he didn't look up to see her expression. He repeated, 'I said I need some water.'

'I am sorry, sir, I presume I can't,' replied the young lady bluntly.

Surprised, the King looked up and said, 'What's wrong? I am requesting for some water!'

'You are ordering me, sir. Please say "please" to help me serve you, sir,' replied the young lady.

The King still did not understand the issue. A little annoyed, he asked, 'Young lady, I'm thirsty. I need to drink now. And I hope you know who I am. I also hope you understand that it is your duty to serve the passengers.'

'I know my duty, sir, but I am not here to take your orders. You can request me for a glass of water but you cannot order me around, sir. And please mention "please".'

Realizing his mistake, the King smiled and said, 'I'm extremely sorry, ma'am. May I have a glass of water please?'

The young lady replied, 'Sure, sir, now you can.' Then she added, 'Sir, I know that you are not only a first-class passenger but also one of the seniormost employees of this airline. Your request is an order, even if you make it politely. I am here to make your journey better, sir, not to take orders. I hope you will not misunderstand me, sir.'

The King nodded, indicating that she was right. Polite and well-behaved, the King knew well that he had not meant to order the young lady but that she had misread his communication and felt dejected. The King learnt the lesson and travelled happily ever after.

'Thank you', 'please' and 'sorry' are some of the truly great words in the English dictionary, when used with sincerity. Let us thank our parents for teaching us these words, and helping us understand their true meanings.

Till a few months ago, back in college, you were among friends all the time. Probably, 'please', 'sorry' or 'thank you' did not matter to you much. But now, with colleagues at work, these are very important. You must appreciate others and show your gratitude. These are little gestures that can propel your journey through your career.

For instance, please say thank you when someone helps you, even when the office boy serves you a cup of tea.

Please remember that he has done his job by serving you tea, which is going to help you freshen up and work better. Please say sorry if you sincerely feel apologetic. There is nothing wrong in accepting your mistake. Humility is appreciated more than arrogance in the corporate world. Please wish people good morning as you enter the office; after all, you will be there with them for the next nine hours, if not more. Please wish people good night when you leave the office; after all, you will meet them again the next day.

These are some basic courtesies that our parents emphasized all the time, but we forgot quickly as we grew up. Why don't we refresh our memories, and practise this politeness ourselves, so that we can be better teachers in the future? Let us not ignore these great lessons. Rather, let us build on them.

***

Mr Chatterjee looked at his watch and said, 'Folks, it is time for lunch. I will stop here today. I do not want to mix up different topics. After lunch, we will reassemble for some time to summarize what we have discussed over the day. Then, next week, we will have a long session.'

We were not hungry yet; we wanted to hear more. I felt bad that we had to stop. I found the sessions so unique. I felt like I had not learnt anything before then! All my education, my coveted degree, never gave me the lessons that Mr Chatterjee taught me in a few hours.

When we reassembled after lunch, Mr Chatterjee said,

'Welcome back! Hope you guys are enjoying my stories.'

We all nodded in agreement.

Mr Chatterjee said, 'I am always nervous when I speak to today's youth. It is the most difficult thing to do.'

We looked surprised. One of us said, 'But, sir, we were good listeners throughout. What makes you think so?'

'That is my point. All of you will absorb what I say. Every one of you will interpret the learning in a different way. I need to ensure that the right message hits you. So it is important that we summarize our learning.'

He then looked at me and said, 'Will you help me please? Let us recap quickly before we call it a day.'

I said, 'Thank you, your highness!'

He smiled and said, 'That was good for those stories. Now I am Vivek Chatterjee, your friend and mentor, one of you.'

I started to sum up the day: 'I think we understood that the corporate world is like a jungle. Just like the jungle has its own unwritten rules, so does the corporate world. Today, we learnt how to get into the jungle. In these early weeks of our career, we need to learn how to adjust to this new world. This will be a new life for us, mostly unknown and unseen. We need to adapt ourselves to this new process, shake off our inhibitions, realign certain mindsets, and empty our minds to learn the new way . . .'

'. . . and that is where your journey will start,' said Mr Chatterjee.

'We need to be open to change, to treat ourselves as students again. We have hit the ground with great expectations and with important goals in mind. We need to work towards them every moment. The biggest challenge will be to accept the change within us, as we need to manage our own expectations. This journey of mental transition requires immense mental strength, and the person who does it the best will be the one at the top of the pyramid,' I added.

I looked at Mr Chatterjee, he nodded, and I continued, 'The onus is on us to understand and adapt ourselves to this new culture. We need to spend half of our life in this jungle, so knowing people here will make our stay better.'

Mr Chatterjee chipped in, 'So please do not be under the impression that knowing your boss is good enough—everyone matters in this jungle.

'We may have left out a few topics today but we can pick them up as we continue our journey. Thank you folks and see you next week, same time, same place. I promise you another exciting day,' said Mr Chatterjee. He got up from his chair and left the club.

As I walked back to my car, I looked up to notice the scorching sun. I laughed and said to myself, 'In the evening, this sun might set for the entire world but, for me, it will always be like this, shining. I have Mr Chatterjee with me. I will ensure that I become a moon to draw light from him, and keep shining throughout. Thank you, your highness!'

SECTION 2

WALKING THROUGH THE JUNGLE

The week that followed was, by far, the best week of my life. The days just zoomed by. The discussion of the previous Saturday occupied my mind, and anticipation of the next session kept me excited. My other colleagues felt the same. We could not stop discussing the stories that Mr Chatterjee had shared with us. No one wanted to miss the next session. We felt as if we were freshers in a college, waiting for the lessons to be showered by Prof. Chatterjee.

The next Saturday, I was the first to arrive at the club. To my surprise, I found Mr Chatterjee sitting by the pool, sipping tea. I greeted him and sat beside him. He smiled and said, 'Ready for the day?'

'Yes, sir!' I replied.

'Thanks for challenging me the other day. I am happy that I accepted your challenge,' he said.

I felt a bit nervous, given that I was the reason he was there that day. After all, he was the group CEO, and I a mere trainee. I said, 'It is so kind of you to give us your time, sir. The whole week, we have waited for this day. I am glad that I did challenge you. Now it appears to me that we had not learnt anything to date which would help us survive in this corporate world.'

'Not true! You have learnt everything, or you would not be sitting next to me today. I am just putting all your learning together and giving it a "corporate shape".'

In some more time, the rest of the group arrived, and we started the day. Mr Chatterjee started speaking: 'Now that we have entered the corporate jungle, we need to stay alive. We must avoid being eaten up by other animals. So, to start with, we will speak about what the corporate world would expect from you, and what you will need to keep yourself breathing. Let us talk about certain dos first.'

DOS

Understand the expectations from you

I never see what has been done; I only see what remains to be done.—The Buddha

Once upon a time, there was a young man who hated the King, his boss at his organization. He had all the reasons to dislike the King. The young man was intelligent and hard-working, but, in spite of his serious efforts, he was unable to meet the King's expectations. Day by day, the young man was getting frustrated. He tried his best, met each deadline, yet he knew that the King was not happy with his performance.

This had never happened to him before. In his college days, he was the top student, always excelling at his studies. Interestingly, during the campus interview, he had rejected this job offer. But then, this very King had persuaded him for hours to join his company. However, things changed once the young man was a part of the company—he felt that the King never appreciated his efforts.

The picture became clearer during his first appraisal, when the King formally expressed his dissatisfaction over his performance. The King said, 'Young man, I had expected a little more from you.'

He felt miserable since this was the first failure of his life. The King was a man of few words, and his statement made the young man nervous. He did not ask further; instead, he promised himself to work harder. He said, 'Your highness, I will work even harder and will ensure that you are happy with my work in my new assignment.' The King smiled.

Over the next six months, he worked even harder. But at the time of the next appraisal, the feedback was no different. The King repeated, 'I had expected a little more from you.'

Yet, surprisingly, this time the King gave him a good rating and increment despite that comment. That the King was still not happy with his performance was a shock to the young man and the discussion shattered his confidence.

He wanted to clear the air and met the King again. He asked, 'Your highness, I tried everything, stressed myself out to the hilt . . . I want to understand what went wrong with my performance this time.'

The King said, 'When I requested you to join us, I knew that you were brilliant. I did your reference check myself and spoke to your professors; everybody told me that you would be an asset to the company. So, I never equated you with other employees. In my mind, you are to deliver much more than any normal employee. That was my expectation. There is no doubt that you worked hard and did what you were asked you to do, but I expected something more.'

'But, your highness, you should have told me this before.'

'I agree that we need to express expectation in a transparent way. The lesser the ambiguity, the better it is. But, in reality, we seldom speak out all our expectations, and that is where the problem begins. Even if I had told you what I expected of you, a few things would remain unstated. The skill is to understand and deliver the unspoken.'

'In that case, your highness, I do not deserve such a good rating or the increment! You did not punish me for not meeting your expectation. Why is that?'

'I did not since your performance was far better than others' on the stated expectation. I know that I did not define everything well; therefore I have no right to penalize you. During the earlier appraisal, I did indicate my dissatisfaction and wanted you to pick up the clue. You failed. Many bosses may not be so generous. You need to anticipate the unstated, and that will be the proof of your smartness.'

The young man received a very important lesson of his life. He lived happily ever after.

A job description can be deceptive; in fact, it can be the biggest deterrent to your career. What we need to understand is that the company's expectations are always greater than the declared objective. You are supposed to deliver what you are told; but everyone else will also deliver the barest minimum—so how will you be different?

If you deliver only what you are told, you become just another performer in the bunch. However, since you have decided to race ahead of the others, you need to deliver something more, something that is unstated. The trick is to understand the unstated yet expected objective.

A corporate comprises people from various backgrounds. Their ways of communication differ. Some of them will state expectations explicitly; some will prefer to hold on to their ideas; some will expect you to understand for yourself; and some will balance out all these approaches. There is no single formula to discover what is expected of you. A good performer always delivers what is stated, so the expectation grows further. Many people will expect you to deliver more than the stated—seniors, peers, even juniors. The more clearly we understand that, the better is our chance to excel.

Each move you make sets the expectations in others' minds. It may not always be through a written or verbal communication; expectations can change through certain actions that you or they have performed unknowingly. They can be changed because of your past performance. They can be based on the perception you have created in others' minds. First, it is important for you to find out what is expected of you, and this includes the unstated expectations. You need to be clear on this aspect every moment, so that you can deliver results effectively.

If, at any time, you feel that the expectation from you is unreasonable, please reason it out. No one will do that for you. At the end of the day, you need to manage each of the expectations from you. It is always better to counter a challenge upfront than fail the expectation later. If you manage expectations upfront, it will be clear to both sides. The other side should know what to expect and when to expect it. Be realistic in your approach. If, at any time, you feel that you may not be able to meet the expectation, please communicate this to the other side and agree with the new norms. The case may be that even after a discussion, your request is not accepted—fair enough. At least you will know what action and resources you need now to meet the expectation. The better you manage expectations of stakeholders, the easier will be your growth to the top.

In several corporate workshops, the speaker starts by asking, 'What do you expect out of today's workshop?' We all speak out our expectations. The speaker notes them down, and, at the end of the day, he or she usually revisits the points. In most cases, it is evident that he or she has done a good job by meeting those expectations. Yet, everybody does not leave the workshop in the same frame of mind. Some go back happy, others dejected. The reason is simple—though we had stated our expectations and the speaker met them, we had a few unstated expectations in our minds. If those are not met, we feel something is missing.

Similarly, in any corporate office, everything will never be defined. You need to master the art of knowing the unknown and delivering it. The onus to deliver is on you.

Agree on the ground rules

You have to learn the rules of the game. And then you have to play better than anyone else.—Albert Einstein

Once upon a time, there was a young man who joined the corporate world. Unlike many young people of his age, he had experienced unlimited freedom when he was growing up. From a very young age, he had developed an independent mind and was used to taking his own decisions. His parents never stopped him or curtailed any decision he took. Nor did they ever pressurize him regarding his studies. He didn't follow any routine, didn't need to explain his actions to anyone. Yet, this young man had enough sense of responsibility, and thus he excelled throughout his academic career.

This young man hated to be guided as much as he hated to be questioned. He hated any reviews by his boss, the King. In fact, within a few months of joining the corporate world, the walls of corporate rules stifled him and he felt suffocated. Life became a pain, since he had to be answerable to someone or the other nearly every day. The King too was upset with him, as the young man never kept the King informed about the progress of any job assigned to him. Fed up with his behaviour, the King scheduled two weekly meetings with him for a formal review. Nothing changed—the young man skipped most of them. One day, the King confronted him and demanded, 'Why don't you come for the weekly review meetings?'

The young man replied, 'I think they are a waste of time.'

The King never expected such a blunt reply. He asked, 'Why do you feel so?'

The young man replied, 'Your highness, I am responsible enough to deliver my job on time, and I always deliver it perfectly. I do not want anyone to supervise me.'

'But I am responsible for your actions too. Don't you think it is your job to keep me appraised? These meetings will help you seek my guidance on any matter.'

'Not really,' answered the young man. 'I am a grown-up. I know what is right for me and for the organization. Leave it to me and you will not regret it.'

The King thought for a while and then decided to give it a try. He said, 'Young man, I respect your thinking process, but let us agree on some ground rules. Once I assign you a job, please discuss it with me and agree on the expectations. I do not want any mismatch between what you expect from a job and what the company needs. I hope that is fine with you.'

Relieved, the young man agreed to the king's proposal. And he lived happily ever after.

There are so many different stakeholders you need to manage—your investors, your customers, your peers, your bosses, your subordinates, your suppliers, your team. All of them are equally important for you to succeed. How will you manage them unless you agree on certain ground rules?

The corporate world is about shared responsibility—we all know that by now. Most of us are dependent on others, hence everyone's delivery is crucial for shared goals and team success. Thus, it is critical to know the ground rules and let others know certain basics you would like to follow. The onus is on you to get these rules communicated and established. Everyone around is different, with diverse work styles, expressions and expectations. These little differences are what make this world so interesting.

The first step is for you to be transparent and ensure that everybody around knows your way of working well. The lesse we keep others guessing, the easier life will be for everybody. Many people would advise you not to be open with others, to keep them guessing—to retain the X-factor. I disagree. I think it is easier to be a difficult person, driven by your own priorities, but that is detrimental to the people around you as well as your own career. You need to challenge this orthodoxy and move forward with an open mind. Let people know you well and understand you better. Please do not allow ambiguity to rule. It will only harm your reputation and affect your speed of delivery. Life is great when you are among people who understand your way of life.

Adapt yourself to a situation

Our very survival depends on our ability to stay awake, to adjust to new ideas, to remain vigilant and to face the challenge of change.—Martin Luther King Jr

Once upon a time, there was a young man who was the only child of the CEO of a multinational. He was born in London, brought up in Frankfurt, and, when his father decided to return to India, he completed his education in India. He got into a premier engineering college and followed it up with an MBA from a premier management institute.

He was a normal young man who loved his guitar, jeans and T-shirts. He was well behaved, respected his elders and excelled at whatever he did. He loved his father but found him boring, especially as he was always dressed in formal attire. He often argued over this but could never win—his father explained to him that it was the ethics of his organization and he could not violate certain unwritten rules. His young mind could not understand this fact, since he had little exposure to the corporate world.

Soon this young man had to appear for his first job interview. He was in a dilemma, because his college required him to wear a suit for the interview. He argued with the dean, but the dean did not budge. The institute was very strict on the interview dress code; after all, it affected their image. If he had to get a job, he had no option but to follow the rule. Finally, he appeared for the interview wearing a suit borrowed from a friend. He felt uncomfortable. In the few hours that he was in formal clothes, he felt so claustrophobic that he decided never to wear them again.

Ironically, this interview led to him being selected for the job. It was probably the best offer in the campus selection. The job was at an investment banking company, and formal dress was mandatory with the job.

The young man, being brilliant in all respects, was high

on confidence. He knew that his work would speak for itself and decided to ignore the dress code. He worked hard every day, but continued to wear his jeans and T-shirt. He shaved only when he wanted, had long hair and often sported a ponytail.

Over the next few years, despite all his efforts, this young man did not progress much in his career. His 'different' approach towards corporate life was not liked by many. He was counselled by his seniors but he fought for his belief. He made it clear that his efficiency did not get affected by the way he dressed; he was delivering more than what was expected of him—where was the problem? His logic was irrefutable, but soon he started being ignored for important client meetings. Over time, he became a back-office boy who churned out all relevant information for a meeting, but was never there to discuss it. He never lived happily ever after.

The corporate atmosphere demands a certain way of life, which is very different from college life. There are certain accepted practices, which we all need to follow. For example, barging into a friend's hostel room is usually acceptable— unless he is in deep conversation with his girlfriend—but barging into a senior's office without knocking is not at all acceptable! Walking into class in college in your slippers may be acceptable but can you imagine yourself walking into an office meeting without shoes?

It is impossible to list these rules as they differ from company to company, country to country, even city to city. The challenge is that, in corporate life, every day matters and every interaction counts. You are judged at every moment; you need to manage impressions all the time.

Please don't think that the only thing that matters is your behaviour with seniors, clients and customers. In the corporate world, everyone around is an opinion-maker. Everyone will have a view about you that may affect your career in some way or the other. Hence, it is not about the right behaviour with an individual alone; we need to respect the corporate culture and adapt to it.

The problem is that no one teaches us how to behave in a corporate set-up. You are supposed to learn it on your own. Observe the people you respect, mix with the people who can mentor you, follow them. This can be a good starting point. You will certainly get to observe certain traits in them, which you would like to adopt.

Impressions are long-lasting. When the young man appeared for the interview, he was dressed to suit the company culture. In any case, he was brilliant, so bagging that coveted job was a cakewalk for him. But then, things changed when he decided not to follow organizational protocol any more. People often believe that the way one conducts himself reflects the way one thinks. The underlying rebellion in this young man's nature was evident to all when he decided not to follow office protocol.

With the economy growing at a faster pace, you have enough options in hand. Hence you must choose to be part of a culture that suits you, or you should have the mental flexibility to adapt to a new culture. The young man's style would probably have worked well in a different industry where casual attire and ponytails are accepted, even appreciated.

Some jobs require intensive client interaction. We need to suit both the company's and the client's unwritten rules. Perhaps when an unshaven, jeans-clad guy with a ponytail puts forth a creative brand idea to a client, it is acceptable. Similarly, when a person in formal suit and tie puts forward a million-dollar investment proposal to a client, the client may feel that it is thought through and hence more acceptable. It has nothing to do with individual brilliance—it has everything to do with the corporate mindset.

There is no reason for all these so-called rules, to be honest, but that is the corporate culture we all live in. Initially, it may be hard to accept but that's how the corporate world works. Your first few years are not the time to rebel against the culture of the company. They are the time to learn, to familiarize, to adapt. The young man failed miserably at this.

Meet deadlines

A goal is a dream with a deadline.—Napoleon Hill

Once upon a time, there was a King who headed the HR department of an organization. The King was working on a project to prepare an induction manual for newcomers. It was a global project, and the King was under pressure to complete it on time.

The King handed over the project to the most brilliant young man in his department, requesting him to deliver it by the end of the third week. The young man had joined the company barely a few months ago, fresh out of college. He exuded confidence, and agreed to finish the project before time.

The King calculated and guessed that, even if the young man took a day or two more, he would still have a few days before submission to review the manual himself. He inquired every now and then about the progress, and each time his brilliant employee assured him that the progress was good, and the job would be finished on time.

At the end of the third week, when the King called for a formal review, he realized that the project was not even half-done. He was astonished. He lost his cool and asked, 'Young man, why the hell was this not done?'

The brilliant employee replied casually, 'I got busy with other work. I didn't get time to concentrate. Moreover, it is a global project and I am working in a way to deliver a perfect manual. That is why it is taking a longer time.'

The King was appalled to realize that the young man hadn't understood the importance of the deadline in the least. He thought for a while and summoned a young woman who had joined the department from a reputed consulting firm a few months ago. The King explained the situation to her, and said, 'I need your help. I do not know how, but you need to help me tide over this situation.'

The young woman agreed to take up the assignment. She delivered it punctually at the end of the next week.

The King asked the young woman to explain how she could meet such a stiff deadline. She explained, 'Your highness, I know the importance of deadlines. I am used to them. I also knew that I had only one week's time to finish a job for which four weeks were assigned originally. I estimated the number of pages I needed to write to complete the manual in seven days, and then divided the task per day. I was then clear about the challenge in hand. That is the reason I am standing here proudly. It does not matter if I am working for an external client or my own boss. Deadlines are deadlines. I need to deliver, every time.'

The King smiled and rewarded the young woman suitably. And they lived happily ever after.

When you accept a deadline, it's a promise you make to others as well as to yourself. Please take it as a commitment from you, on behalf of your team. People judge you when you deliver or don't deliver your promise. Please remember that your reputation as well as your career will be at stake, if you miss your commitments regularly.

In college life, if you don't submit your assignments on time, the loss is yours—you lose marks, you lose grades. No one else suffers. But, in the corporate world, you work in a team for an organization. All your actions have a multiplier effect and thus the loss will be for many. Corporate life is often like a relay race—if you don't pass on the baton, the next person will not be able to run. Others will suffer if you default on your commitments.

Deadlines can be a toll on you but you need to manage them. How often have you heard: 'Deadlines are deadlines. I do not care. You need to deliver!'? If not yet, just wait. Soon this will become a way of your life, whatever field you work in.

Look at the positive side—this helps you set a goal and work towards it. It can be satisfying when you meet it. At times you may fail, and those can be trying times. But as long as you have given the job the best of your zeal and planning abilities, others will understand and probably pardon you. But you should never lose sight of your deadlines. Set up a calendar for yourself, monitor it regularly, and ask yourself every time if you need to tweak it a little. That is what the young woman did when the King assigned her the job. The activity chart on her desk helped her judge her own progress every day. And that is how she succeeded. Realizing the importance of deadlines will help you make it a habit to meet your deadlines every time.

Promise what you will deliver

The only real failure in life is not to be true to the best one knows.—The Buddha

Once upon a time, there was a King who was the head of a business unit of a multinational. He reported to the worldwide head of business. That year, the King had a unique problem to tackle. The problem was of managing an over-delivery—by year-end, the company had delivered much higher profits than the King had promised to his parent company at the beginning of the year.

The Minister, the company's CFO, was very happy with the result. The King felt elated, since he had actually delivered much more than what he had promised. He thought he had done a wonderful job. But he did not know that, behind his back in the corporate headquarters, people laughed at him, because they felt he was inefficient and did not understand the business. They even doubted his integrity.

The issue did not end there. The King's business was a significant part of the global business done by the company, and thus it did affect its overall results. The board of directors pulled up the global head of the company and questioned his acumen about the predictability of the business. He had no answer to offer. He, in turn, charged the King for his non-transparent approach. The King was called to the global headquarters to explain the results.

The King, who was not too savvy with financial numbers, depended on the Minister for them. He trusted the Minister and relied on his projections. He, too, had foreseen a little over-delivery but he never thought that it would snowball into a serious issue. During the meeting, the global head of the company told the King, 'I am not happy with your results. You have put me in a difficult position.'

'But, your highness, I have delivered 200 per cent of what I had promised at the start of the year,' replied the King, surprised.

'Yes, and that is my problem. I now doubt if my businesses are in safe hands. These results imply that either you knew that you would deliver this much extra, or, and I'm sorry to say this, that your people do not know their business,' said the global head.

'But, your highness, I am still surprised. Instead of blaming me, you should be happy with such a great result!' replied the King.

'This approach does not help. If I had these predictions in advance, I could have advised you to run the business differently. We could have taken several decisions that I delayed for the want of funds.'

The global CEO thought for a while and said, 'Please have a word with your Minister and advise him. He should have guided you better. I think we need a better CFO.'

The King took the blame upon himself and said, 'It is not the Minister's fault. I had advised the Minister to submit those numbers.'

'Then be careful in the future,' advised the global head.

Back in his office, the King had a long chat with the Minister, to explain the situation to him and advise him to be more transparent. Unfortunately, the Minister did not realize the importance of the right projections, and continued to work the way he was used to. The problem of over-delivery continued, and soon the King had no option but to ask the Minister to leave the company. The King got a new Minister, and they lived happily ever after.

In the corporate world, most people believe in 'Under-promise and over-deliver'. I choose to disagree with this concept. It has its positive and negative aspects. In no circumstances should you deliver less than what you had promised. But then you need to be transparent and convey the right message.

In the corporate world, every activity or decision is followed or preceded by another. Hence, both under- and over-delivery have their own connotations. The right thing is to promise right and deliver accordingly.

Let us believe in transparency. Put on the table what the line of sight is today and what the aspiration is. Let all forces converge to help you achieve a greater result than promised. In an approach like this, in some cases, you may fail, but then, in most cases, the pleasure of winning will be genuine.

For instance, you should always strive to complete a task before the deadline, or deliver a result higher than the target, and factor in a margin of safety in your calculations before agreeing on a promise. However, knowingly keeping a 'large cushion' for yourselves is a dangerous game; you may be perceived as someone who is not confident to declare stretch goals.

Under-promising and over-delivery leave a lot of doubt in others' minds. People at the other side of the table may think, 'If the task was as complicated as communicated to me, how come it was delivered earlier than the plan?', or 'Do these guys even know their business? How come they always deliver more than their sales targets?', or 'I doubt their integrity. I'm sure they knew it earlier. They are a bunch of sandbaggers!'

Then, the next time you deliver before the promised time, these people will think, 'What's new? I knew it.' By then, the charm as well as the trust is gone. There is a thin line between being prudent and being dishonest. You must tread this line carefully for continued success. Therefore, over-deliver purely by effort, not by design.

The CFO, even after being told by the King, did not understand the implication of a wrong promise. He still believed that what he did was right, since he has delivered more. He had to quit the job since he believed in what he did, and did not see anything wrong in his style. It had by then become a habit. He did not like to live differently.

Thus a 'wrong promise' is a habit that can easily turn into a disease, unless you learn to control it. It gets into your everyday life. You need to talk to yourselves in your initial days and master the art of promising right. You can then live peacefully, and your credibility will never be at stake in this jungle.

Deliver every time

In delay, we waste our lights in vain, like lamps by day.
—William Shakespeare

Once upon a time, there was a young man who headed the projects division of a construction company. In a few years, he had earned a great name for himself. He was known to deliver every task on time. Even at that young age, he was becoming one of the most promising names for project management in the country.

Now, this young man was upset. He was unhappy with one of his current projects. It was delayed by a few weeks and the review with the King, the CEO of the projects division, was due the following week. He was visibly disturbed.

On the review day, the young man was to present the status of all his projects. As all the projects, except one, were meeting deadlines, his team suggested that he started the presentation with the projects that were on time, and slipped in the delayed project towards the end. The young man smiled and went back to his office to prepare his presentation.

At the presentation, to the surprise of all, he started with the bad news. The King was upset and challenged the young man. Though he had enough justifications for the delay, the young man admitted that the fault was his, for he had not spent much time detailing this particular project. The King expressed his annoyance and warned him to be more diligent in the future.

After that, the young man presented his other projects, which were all—to the King's surprise and delight—greatly ahead of schedule. At the end, the King was pleased and said, 'I am sorry for being upset with you. I should not have reacted at the delay on just one project.'

'Your highness,' replied the young man, 'I did not mind your reaction. I knew I was at fault.'

'But, young man, you could have presented the bad news at the end, after I had reviewed all your good work. Then I would've readily understood that one project as the exception.'

'It is not that this idea did not cross our minds, but I deliberately chose not to do that.'

'But why? Why did you invite trouble for yourself?'

'I have seen many of my bosses in my early corporate life go that way. I wondered why they felt happy to hide their failures. When I observed them from a distance, I realized that they were wrong. Those first few years taught me that instead of hiding my failures, I must concentrate on the end result. I am not upset that you have scolded me; I am upset that I have not delivered my promise. I am running against myself.'

The King smiled and said, 'You have an unimpeachable track record; one failure should not bother you at all.'

'It bothers me, your highness. I need to keep my track record on track. That is the reason I wanted to show you my failure, so that I could challenge myself even more.'

The King said, 'I need many more young men like you in the system. I am proud of you.' And they lived happily ever after.

Many people take too much pride in their past laurels. In the corporate world, the past is past. It is fast forgotten. You are as good as what you are today. Past achievements will help you stay afloat, give you the confidence to move to the next achievement and build your reputation, but that's all they will do. No one will care to know that you were 'so good' in the past when you have failed to deliver in the present.

You need to perform relentlessly. You need to apply

all possible methods to meet deadlines and honour commitments. That is how you are judged as performers. You are like stage actors or singers, who cannot goof up in their performance and then say, 'Remember last time I sang or acted so well!' Do you think the public that has waited for hours to be entertained by them will accept this excuse?

All of us are successful because we have performed well in the past, but after that many people take success for granted. Thus, many managers quickly turn into incompetent managers. The most common reason is complacency.

Let us agree that everybody in the corporate world is led by a target. The type and size of target may differ but everybody has a target to meet. It is a necessary evil. Even a single miss can cost you a fortune. People will watch you for some time, give you some leeway, but no one will pardon you for constantly not delivering results. You are paid to be successful every single time.

You can deliver every time if we demonstrate a strong commitment to win every battle. The basic understanding that even one failure can put your career behind others is good enough to make you deliver every time. You need to have high ambition, self-motivation, self-esteem, and the zeal to move ahead. Like in a game of golf, you have to challenge yourself, play against yourself, keep on demanding more from yourself. You better learn this lesson in your initial days.

Take every conversation seriously

Attitude is a little thing that makes a big difference.
—Winston Churchill

Once upon a time, there was a King who was the CEO of a large corporation. The King was looking for a bright young talent to become his executive assistant. It was an important position, and the candidate had to possess high levels of maturity, commitment and integrity since he or she would be privy to all the King's strategies or decisions for the company. Some of the ministers advised the King that he should pick up a person from the latest batch of management trainees, who had recently graduated into their roles. The King agreed, since he too wanted new talent who would bring in fresh perspective to the business.

It was a coveted position for any young person. He would rub shoulders with the who's who in the company, get information ahead of others, travel with the King and accompany him to all important meetings. Past record showed that anyone who donned this role moved ahead of his batchmates, merely because of the exposure it provided.

The King shortlisted two candidates from the latest batch. The annual off-site conference for managers was under way. The King decided to attend this meeting, in order to watch both these young men closely, at work and away from it, before taking the final call. He believed that his executive assistant would play a big role even away from regular office work, like in corporate parties, interacting with senior leaders within and outside the company, in conferences and so on.

That evening, after the conference, the company organized cocktails and dinner. It was a happy occasion for all the employees, since the company had just announced its last-quarter results, recording the highest-ever profit and sales in its history. That the King too was part of the celebration made them happier. The King enjoyed himself, spending time with most of the managers present. In fact, he was the last to leave the party.

A fitness freak, the King never missed a day of exercise even when he travelled. Wanting to spend some more time with the two young men, he requested them to join him for a gym session the next morning. Both of them agreed to meet him at 6 a.m. at the fitness centre.

While one of them walked into the gym at the agreed time, attired properly, the other did not show up. Later, when the King finished his workout and was leaving for his room, he saw the other young man walking towards the gym in his night suit. His excuse was that he had an urgent phone call to attend and hence could not join the King at the gym. The next day, the King announced that the first gentleman would be his executive assistant. The other young man never lived happily ever after.

We are not here to discuss if the King was right in his decision. The second young man had agreed to the King's request the previous night, so he should have honoured his commitment. Honouring a commitment is an integral part of corporate culture. You are not among friends any more; you are among professionals, who are part of the fat race. They watch every step you take. When the second young man decided not to honour his commitment, he didn't realize what an opportunity he could miss. He didn't tale the King's request seriously, thinking it was just a casual remark made after a few drinks.

He was probably used to such behaviour in the past. Perhaps he often did not turn up for a morning walk, even after promising his friends. But things have changed for him, and he did not adapt to the change. A missed commitment in the college days may not be so costly, but now every moment counts, since each and every moment is a moment for a new opportunity. In this case, he missed a golden opportunity, which would have probably taken him much ahead of others in his career.

The 'chalta hai' attitude will not work for you any more. It is important that you change your attitude and take every conversation seriously, the moment you start walking through the corporate jungle. The faster you learn and change yourselves, the better will be your journey through this jungle.

Keep learning on the job

The only source of knowledge is experience.—Albert Einstein

Once upon a time, there was a young man who joined the corporate world. He had a brilliant academic career.

He was always ahead of his classmates, and his teachers loved him. He was so brilliant that he was often invited to teach his own class. By virtue of his brilliance, he got into a premier management institute, and soon joined one of the world's leading banks. After a year of training, he was confirmed in his job and assigned to the retail banking division, a job he had always sought. He was confident about taking up the new challenge, boosted by his impeccable educational record.

Banking was a new industry to this young man; he needed to learn a lot. But he knew he was brilliant, so he decided to learn the trade on his own. He asked neither his colleagues for help nor his seniors for guidance. He learned through books. And thus mastered all the theories, not knowing fully their practical usage.

Even though the young man projected a know-it-all attitude and an image of being in control, his lack of knowledge soon became evident to all. After a while, his colleagues laughed at his back. People started to avoid him. Day by day, his performance dipped. One day, the King, his boss, called him and reprimanded him thoroughly for his non-performance. The young man felt miserable but didn't get demoralized; he was determined to prove his brilliance to the King. He tried harder, but nothing changed. He was soon termed a failure.

At the annual appraisal, the King called him again and said, 'Most things in the corporate world do not happen by the book. It's a practical world—your past laurels and scores will not help you here. You have to start afresh and relearn. You need to ask people, be with them, observe them closely. Think of yourself as a student again. That is the only way to go. There's nothing wrong in admitting that you do not know something.'

The young man still did not learn. His ego did not allow him to admit that there was something he did not know. After a few months, the King counselled him again, but the young man decided not to take the King's advice. In a few months, the King asked the young man to leave the job. They never lived happily ever after.

You have just started your journey in this corporate world; you are not expected to know everything. Admitting that you need to learn will actually help you settle down faster. This is the best time for you to grab as much knowledge as you can. No one will question your intelligence if you admit that you do not know something. This is your chance to understand the business from all possible angles.

Think about yourself when you joined pre-school. Think of your journey to earn your degree. Was not that gradual? Did you know all the fancy management jargon when you were in middle school? No, right? Every year, when you entered a new class, a new syllabus was offered to you. You had books, teachers, notes to guide you. It was a journey you undertook to reach where you are today. You learnt at every step. You learnt, because you were open to learning, asking questions, absorbing new knowledge. You were excited about exploring new avenues.

The corporate world is quite similar. You are just a student here and, at this stage, no one expects you to know what—for example—your King knows. The difference between your earlier life and this one is that you do not have a curriculum, assigned teachers, or books to teach you within a time frame. Hence the only way to start is to admit that you need to learn, and then to go for it.

It is just a matter of time before you will know as much as your King knows, but, first of all, open your mind, and create the hunger to know more. Your ego, your past degrees will be of no use unless you become like a sponge and agree to learn on the job from the start of your journey.

Accept mistakes, embrace criticism

Be not ashamed of mistakes and thus make them crimes.
—Confucius

Once upon a time, a young man joined a construction company. He was an engineer and an expert in estimation of project costs. He had only a few years' experience, but, within this short span of time, he had established himself as a master of project costing.

In his new organization, this young man had a very important position. He would prepare the costing for all tender submissions. Before the marketing department submitted any quotation to the client, he had to sign off the document. The King, who was the marketing head, and other senior members of the organization depended on him. They knew that any mistake made by this young man could cause immense damage to the company. The position was so critical that the King himself had got involved in the recruitment process, and selected this young man personally.

The young man established himself in the new company quite well and quickly. The King was happy with his initial performance.

Interestingly, the young man loved to experiment with new methods. The downside of this was that he never disclosed to others that he was trying out a new method. As luck would have it, he was always successful in his experiments and the company always benefited. Thus, his efforts were always appreciated. In one project, however, a new technique boomeranged. He made a blunder in his estimation, and the company lost a large order.

The King was upset and blamed the marketing department for not submitting the right quotation. Surprised at this loss, the young man decided to analyse his own work. To his dismay, he discovered that his own experiment had been the reason for the loss of the order. He felt more dejected because the King had blamed the others in the team, not realizing that he was the culprit. He went up to the King, and confessed.

The King listened to him, smiled and said, 'I, too, was bothered that we lost the order. I felt miserable and thus blamed our marketing folks. But now all my worries are gone. I am happy to see that you have the urge to analyse yourself and the conviction to admit your mistake. You could have kept quiet, since the blame was already laid on the others. But you did not. I like your sincerity. I firmly believe that if you work, you will make mistakes—only if you don't, you won't. We certainly need more people like you. On your journey to the top, some people may criticize you for your mistakes; but take them in your stride, embrace them. Positive criticism will always help you to sharpen your skills. Hence my request to you is to keep trying out new methods—one mistake or two don't make a difference. In the long run, this will help the business.'

The young man felt better. The King added, 'Please don't feel bad! I want you to feel like a winner. I want a victor to go out from my office. Smile, and move on. You have many more mistakes to make in the future!'

The young man smiled and left. And they lived happily ever after.

Mistakes are part of everyone's lives. As long as you live, be it in the corporate world or elsewhere, mistakes will occur. It is vital for you to understand how to deal with them. No one makes a mistake for the sake of making it. It happens, though the intention is to deliver a perfect result. Thus, most mistakes are unintentional. Hiding a mistake is not the solution. The past is past—it cannot be undone. Crying over spilt milk will only waste time and energy. It is important to accept a mistake, understand the cause, learn from it, and move on.

The corporate world is a competitive place, and mistakes, once unearthed, will raise a few eyebrows, spark off some juicy discussions, leading to direct or indirect criticism. You must learn to deal with such critics, take their comments positively and move ahead.

With experience, you will learn to detect early signals that may lead to undesirable results. We must know what to change in ourselves or in the system to avoid such issues, and how to work better to avoid slip-ups in the future. But you should always own up and accept your mistakes. It is always appreciated. What the young man did was probably the best thing to do—he went to the King and accepted his fault. It showed his conviction and integrity as a human being. On his part, the King appreciated the fact that the young man's intention was not to do wrong. He also appreciated that the young man realized and admitted his mistake. Most often, such a gesture is well-appreciated—the outcome is immaterial. You need to clear your conscience. When you are ready to correct yourself, who cares about the outcome?

Life will go on. At worst, you may have to find another King and move on. But it is important to be true to oneself. Hence, let us get into this noble habit of accepting our mistakes. It is the right thing to do and you must practise this trait from the day your enter the jungle.

Offer solutions

It is not because things are difficult that we do not dare, it is because we do not dare that things are difficult.—Seneca

Once upon a time, there was a King who was the operations head of a company. The company was going through a crisis, its sales were dipping and profit was at an all-time low. Moreover, the company had also recently lost market share.

The Board of Directors challenged the King, since he was missing his target every month. The King tried everything, from new strategies to new products to new campaigns, but nothing worked. He was losing confidence. Disappointed with his own performance, he was on the verge of quitting, to pursue another career.

One evening, the King was chatting with a friend. He explained the issue to his friend, and reasoned why he was contemplating leaving his job. The friend listened carefully and asked, 'I can understand that the results are not good. I can appreciate your agony. But does your team know that you are facing such a big problem?'

The King replied, 'Yes, all of them know. We have a weekly meeting to discuss the issues.'

The friend asked, 'What happens at that meeting?'

'My team reports problems to me and I offer solutions. I have started a new report called "The Problem Grid", where everybody reports their problems to me by Friday evening. My assistant consolidates them, and we all look at the problem at our meeting on Monday.'

Even more interested now, the friend asked, 'When did you start this system?'

'About a year ago, just when we started facing problems.'

The friend smiled and said, 'Now please explain to me how exactly this is carried out.'

'I give my team the solutions. The team works on them. By the weekend, they report the results, and we discuss the problems again on Monday.'

'Is the list of problems growing every week?'

'Yes,' said the King, 'but how can you guess that?'

The friend laughed and said, 'I have good news for you. You do not need to look for a new job.'

'What do you mean?'

'Just take my suggestion. Make the "problem grid" a "solution grid", and ask each member to put up a possible solution to the problem he or she reported. They know their job the best, and simply giving you the problem to solve will not help anybody. They need to offer you their solutions as well. Once you have the list of probable solutions, ask your team to resolve them before the next meeting.'

The King asked sarcastically, 'And what will happen if I change my grid?'

'Simple! Your people will start taking responsibility for their issues. Anyone who is not willing to offer a solution will be phased out automatically.'

The King pondered for a moment and asked, 'What makes you so sure that your suggestion will work?'

The friend did not reply. He smiled and said, 'Try it, and let us talk again after a few months.'

The King changed the system, and introduced the concept of 'the Solution Grid'. The results were amazing. Soon the list of problems started to dwindle, as people started to find their own solutions. The company began to thrive again. The King did not have to leave the job, and he lived happily ever after.

Everyone has his problems, as does every company. Managers are appointed to solve these problems and guide the team through crises. You are the people who have been appointed to suggest solutions to problems. Thus, merely reporting a problem is not what is expected from any of you. That method will only delay situation resolution.

I'm not suggesting that you should not report a problem, but you must, at the same time, try to find a possible solution to offer. Any senior would want his juniors to come to him not only with a problem, but also with a possible solution for it. It is always better to analyse and think through a problem and look at possible solutions before running around to simply report the issue. No one gets an early-bird prize for reporting a problem without thinking through for a solution. Every colleague of yours, be it a peer or a junior or a senior, will appreciate someone who has at least tried to work out a solution. It demonstrates care for the company as well as a positive frame of mind. Most problems that appear insurmountable at first probably have a simple solution. The problem with a problem is that you think of it as a problem, and leave it for someone else to solve!

Take a step back, analyse the cause of the problem and ask yourself if there is a solution in it. Often, you would already know how to resolve your problem. You might need help from others and may seek their involvement. In that process, discussions will be healthy and solutions swifter.

It is important for you to make this process a habit from your initial days in a corporate. Nature has given you enough strength to find your own solutions. Why should you depend on others to suggest the way forward?

Secure quick wins

The first man gets the oyster; the second man gets the shell.
—Andrew Carnegie

Once upon a time, there was a smart young man who joined a company's finance team as a management trainee. He settled down fast and learnt well in the first few months. He had a very positive attitude, displayed high energy, and was willing to accept new challenges. Within a few months, he started doing well in his career and made a mark in his seniors' minds.

Around that time, the company launched a high-visibility cost reduction programme, headed by a senior leader. The programme was supported by all functional representatives. The project was run by a project management office (PMO) which was headed by the CFO himself. To manage the PMO efficiently, he needed a bright young mind, and decided to appoint someone from the finance department to keep track of all cost-saving initiatives. This young man was recommended for the job.

The PMO identified several areas for improvement, including communication costs. The team brainstormed, took quotations from different service providers, negotiated rates and finally came out with the recommendation to change the telephone service provider—a simple change that would save the company around 30 per cent of the communication cost. The recommendations were presented to other senior leaders, but no one took a call. The PMO was told that there was a risk associated with changing telephone numbers, and the business might suffer. Hence the initiative was put on hold.

The young man did not like the decision. When he dug further, he discovered that the King, the CEO, was once an employee of the current service provider, and thus no senior leader would take a chance to talk to the King about the proposed change. Everybody knew that the King would not like the decision—the day he had joined the company, he had stated that he valued his former employer and would be loyal to them till the day he would have a mobile phone.

The young man found his opportunity one day, when the King was alone in his office. He walked in and explained the savings opportunity to the King. The King asked, 'But why are you sharing this idea with me? We have formed the PMO to take these decisions.'

The young man said, 'Because I need your approval.'

The King smiled and said, 'Who has told you that you need my approval for such a small decision?'

'I need it as everybody has refused to change the service provider.' The young man reminded the King of his past statement on loyalty.

The King laughed and said, 'Just go ahead. I will keep my old number as my secondary number.'

The young man became an overnight hero and came to be known as the fearless person who could even walk up to the King and suggest a change, if that was good for the company. He was seen as a man with integrity, a person who cared for the company. And he lived happily ever after.

In today's corporate world, new leaders are expected to produce notable results in no time. The pressure on them is quite high. It's not easy to always produce quick results. Many struggle to produce that quick result in the expected time. The confidence shatters, the morale goes down for any individual, especially when your peers have done wonders in no time and you have not. You may not be different.

Identifying quick wins may not be always easy. If it was so easy, then someone would have plucked the opportunity before you. But that is logic; corporate world does not always follow the logic. Hence one is expected to win and that too quickly.

And often it has been proven true that the people who have produced early results are termed as 'bright kids' or the 'leaders of the future'. Simply stated, they have the chance to move ahead of the other 'average/good performing associates'. In fact, if nothing happens, it definitely boosts the person's energy and determination and strengthens his belief that he is the future leader. Thus, like it or not, it is important for you to produce quick results.

Look around, look for that opportunity and look for that option that no one even thought of earlier. That is the best way to secure a great career. This young man's example is quite simple. He sensed the opportunity, believed in the cause. He showed the courage and conviction which many of his peers never explored and senior colleagues refused to own up.

But please be careful. An urge to succeed faster may give you wrong thoughts. Keep that in mind, and never take a dubious way. That is not the idea. It will catch up on you soon. You must find out the unexplored, the un-thought of or even the un-ventured routes to get your results. Trust me, most of these routes are known to all, but may not have been tapped for various reasons. What is important is for you is to be creative. The earlier you tap the opportunity, the better it will be for you.

Get involved

Nothing is interesting, if you are not interested. —Helen MacInnes

Once upon a time, there was a young man who had just joined a company as a management trainee. He had spent his whole life in Kolkata and decided never to move out of the city. Though many of his friends moved out for studies and then took up jobs elsewhere, this young man always managed to stay back. In fact, he gave up his IIT seat and completed his engineering degree from the city, only to be in that city. He completed his engineering studies and landed a job in the city.

His friends, who had to leave the city, often envied him for being able to stay back. He always said, 'I will never leave my city for my career. It is my life; I will decide how to live it.'

He loved his friends and couldn't live a day without the evening 'adda', the informal meeting of friends at the locality where he grew up. He was so attached to his friends that he could sacrifice anything for those evening sessions. He always said, 'These few hours keep me alive.'

His first day at work went off with him sitting in an air-conditioned office, doing nothing but completing formalities and filling forms. He did not like his day. All he did was to wait for the clock to strike 6 p.m.

Around 5 p.m., the HR department called all the management trainees to the conference room for an address by the King, the CEO of the company. The young man hoped that the lecture would end by 6 p.m. He wanted to be on time for his adda. The group waited in the conference hall for a long time, but the King was stuck in another meeting. This meeting would start a bit late. The young man worried that the meeting would stretch beyond the office hours.

After about half an hour, the King arrived, and the meeting started. It was a large group, and by the time everybody finished their introductions, it was already past 6 p.m. It was then time for the King to speak. The young man inquired with the HR person about the expected time for the lecture to be over; she indicated that the session might be over by 7 p.m., and that there was a surprise dinner for the team to be served later.

The young man felt increasingly restless and decided to skip the dinner. Nothing in the meeting registered in his mind; he looked at his watch repeatedly, hoping that the King would finish his lecture early. By the time the King finished, it was 7 p.m. Dinner was announced, to a big round of applause. As drinks were served, all trainees gathered around the King for an informal discussion. The young man did not bother; he slipped past the group and rushed out of the office. The very next day, he was counselled to get more involved in his work. The young man perceived the warning, and promised to give his best to his work. Over time, with the effort and zeal to succeed, he changed himself and lived happily ever after.

Out of many mantras to success, an important mantra is that you need to choose to remain involved. You are in the corporate world by choice, no one had forced you to be there and you thus have the option to leave this fat race. But as you have chosen to be there, people around you expect you to remain involved all the time.

It is not easy. Many times, you will find it boring; your priorities will not match that of the company, your personal commitment or your personal liking will push you to remain aloof from the madness. Those are the moments you need to remain in control of yourself. Take a step back and ask yourself: 'Do I have a choice? Can I stay away from this madness even for a moment? If I choose not to get involved, will I or my company make progress? Will that be beneficial for our team?

Will that help me in my career?' And you will get your own answer.

In short, we need to remain involved as long as we decide to be in the corporate world. In the story, the young man decided not to get involved and was thus not listening to the King. He ignored his invitation to dinner and left the party without even informing the host. He thus showed disrespect and unknowingly gave an impression to the company that he was not interested in the job. That is unacceptable behaviour and hence he was counselled the next day.

Be aware of the power equations

When two elephants fight, it is the grass that gets trampled.
—African proverb

Once upon a time, there was organization known for its high-profile top management. The management team had two fine gentlemen—one headed sales, the other finance. The finance head was perceived to the closest confidant of the King, the CEO. It was widely believed that he was the brain behind the company's success, as the King always took his advice.

The sales head did not like their proximity. Firstly, sales were growing at a record pace. Secondly, the sales head and the finance head had worked in the same company earlier, and there the finance head was junior to him in the hierarchy. But, in this company, though both were vice-presidents, the finance head was practically senior because of his proximity to the King. The sales head also hated it when people spoke about the finance head being groomed to become the next King. It meant that one day he would officially have to report to the finance head, who was once his junior!

There was a young man who worked in the corporate HR. This tension between the two VPs affected his work, as he had to coordinate with both. Any proposal that required both sales and finance approval would invariably go into a loop, as neither of them would agree with the other unless the King mandated it. This young man also respected both individuals, knowing that both were brilliant. However, this ego battle was affecting his performance in a big way; at times, he was even hauled up for under-delivery.

Now, this young man knew that the King too was aware of this issue, but didn't bother to resolve it. The young man couldn't understand why. He sincerely believed that the rift was not good for the organization and finally decided to act on it. When he spoke to his HR head, he got an interesting reply: 'Yes, I am aware of the fact, as is the King. I'd be happy if you didn't talk about it. You are no one to resolve the issue.'

'But sir, it is affecting my career, and my delivery is suffering.'

'That may be the case, but this too is a lesson. You need to know how to tackle delicate situations. I must say that you are doing well, better than I expected. You are learning to live in this new world.'

The young man was surprised. The HR head added, 'Let me share something with you in confidence. Both of them are very senior associates, and we thought they would shed their ego issues and display maturity. Unfortunately, they failed to do so. The King could have resolved this issue months ago, but chose not to. He wanted to give them more time. But they still failed, and I won't be surprised if it hampers their careers. But it is for them to suffer. I suggest that you never come in between two powerhouses, or the only one to suffer would be you. You will be walked over and crushed, before you even realize it.'

The young man understood the message and he lived happily ever after.

When two elephants fight, stay away. You are too small an element in the corporate jungle to stop them. We all know that the corporate hierarchy is like a pyramid—the higher we go, the narrower it gets. Hence, people fight for position, for superiority.

Fights between two senior people are widespread in this corporate world. The reasons can be many. It is not always to secure a position, or to argue for a cause. It can also be just to satisfy their bloated egos. Please do not try to analyse why the ego is so prominent here. It can start with anything, even a trivial issue such as the King visiting one person's room more times in a day than the other person's, or one person getting a higher annual increment than the other.

As a starter, just stay away from the crossfire. Becoming a casualty in such an ugly battle is simply not worth it. Do not discuss these matters with others either; if possible, try to avoid them totally. You never know when two fighting elephants will become best friends and you the fall guy!

The young man did the right thing by talking to his senior. His job was to manage the sales head and the finance head. He could not shy away from that responsibility. He had to deliver what was expected out of him, in any situation. The advice of the HR head helped, and he was lucky to learn the lesson early in his career without becoming a victim.

Walk around

Learn from the whisper, learn from the noise, learn from the quietness and ask yourself why not?—from my book *Why Not . . .! Racing ahead with Mentors*

Once upon a time, there was a young man who started his career as a shop floor engineer. After a few years, when he realized that he was keenly interested in finance, he took a sabbatical to earn a finance degree. Soon after, he was absorbed by the same company in the finance department.

The King, the factory head, observed tremendous improvement in the process of the factory soon after the young man joined. He introduced several checks and balances that helped the factory churn out quality products at a low costs.

The King was certain that the mix of engineering and finance was this young man's advantage. He decided to promote the young man, but before that he wanted to know how he achieved the process improvements in such a short time. Before handing over the letter, he called the young man for an interaction.

The King said, 'Thank you for all your intelligent work. Based on your performance, I have decided to reward you with a promotion.' The King handed over the letter. The young man was extremely pleased and thanked the King. The King asked, 'Before you leave, can you help me understand what you did differently? Did your education help you achieve so quickly what even I could not, with so many senior managers under me?'

The young man proudly said, 'Your highness, I just walked around the factory twice every day.'

'What does that mean?' asked a surprised King.

'It means a lot. My higher education gave me a better understanding of numbers, but that was just a starting point. What worked for me was that walk around the factory. It helped me connect with the right people at the right time, helped me to understand problems better. When I suggested any change, everybody accepted, since those were the problems I identified with them on the shop floor.'

The King asked, 'Tell me more. I'm curious.'

'My degree got me the job I wanted. When I worked as an engineer, I always had a strange feeling that I was not effective. No one took my suggestions seriously. I always felt that I did not impact the business, being on the shop floor. I could never figure out the real reason. I felt that finance would be a better place to influence the business, since I would be in a position to control situations. I was wrong. During my sabbatical, I thought about why I was not effective earlier. I concluded that I was too bookish. I never understood the problems, as I was too bogged down at my desk with my work, and had no relationship with people outside my domain. I failed to connect with people in other departments, and I never had the big picture to support my arguments. When I returned to the company, I changed my work style. Now, I mix with people, talk to others, get their perspectives. It has helped me. People can relate to me. I am acceptable.'

The King felt ashamed. He often lectured his staff, 'Please do not be couch potatoes. Walk around, meet people; it will help you address problems better.' But he seldom practised what he preached.

Soon, the King sent out a circular mandating that every manager take a round of the factory at least once every day. The young man was rewarded further, and they lived happily ever after.

How many hours do you spend in the office? How often do you walk across the floor to another workstation to meet people? Aren't you bored in your seats? Don't you need fresh air? Or do you think that is a waste of time?

If you think that way, you are wrong. Why don't you walk around every now and then, make friends, meet new people, understand them? Trust me, that will make you feel much better, and the best part is that you will learn many new things.

Many of us think that walking around the office is a waste of time. I reiterate that it is the most useful thing you can do to yourself. If you are visible, you are acceptable. Look at what you are doing by simply walking around— you are meeting new people and you are approaching others in their offices to discuss and resolve issues. Isn't that enough for you to garner their support instead of waiting for them to come to your desk?

The young man's regular rounds of the factory helped him add value to the business. This strategy of his made him more acceptable to everyone, and helped him succeed.

**

It was time for a break. Mr Chatterjee said, 'I will stop now. I may have skipped a few "dos" but you will pick those up as you travel though the jungle. It is now time to talk about a few "don'ts". I always say that it is easy to learn the things we need to do but tough to avoid what we must not do. We humans tend to like what is not ours or don't deserve or aren't permitted to do!' We all laughed. Mr Chatterjee said, 'The art is to know them all and still stay away. I promise another interesting session after lunch.'

I rushed to have a quick bite.

DON'TS

'What I am going to talk about now is easier said than done. These are the juiciest attractions of this jungle, and will keep tempting you, making you wonder why you should not partake of them. Often, even unknowingly, you will be dragged into participating in them, but, if you are smart and want to make an impression early in your career, beware of them from the very day you join this new world,' said Mr Chatterjee, as he started our post-break session. He added, 'Your life will be a little dull without these, but let it be. It is better to be careful than regret for ever.'

Avoid gossip in the office

He gossips habitually; he lacks the common wisdom to keep still that deadly enemy of man, his own tongue.—Mark Twain

Once upon a time, there was a young man who joined a low-cost airline. It was his first job; he had taken up the job straight from campus. He had always had a passion for aviation and this job was a dream come true for him. Hardworking and intelligent, the young man quickly became the blue-eyed boy of the King, the CEO of the company.

However, the young man had two problems. He actively participated in any discussion that involved juicy stories and he could not keep secrets. In simple words, he loved office gossip.

Whenever he heard a juicy story, he moved around and spoke to his 'friends', informing them of what he had just heard. He enjoyed spreading stories, as he wanted to be the first to share any news with others. People around him waited for his stories. This trait slowly made him popular among his co-workers, and he started to enjoy his newfound popularity.

The King often wondered how news spread so fast, how decisions taken within four walls reached the competition so rapidly. They were unable to crack the mystery, though. Since the young man was a well-behaved, diligent and intelligent worker, no one doubted his integrity. Interestingly, the young man never felt that he was doing something wrong or going against the company's rules. After all, he was just talking to his best friends who, in turn, were talking to their best friends, and so on.

Life was good for the young man till a rumour spread about the Operations Head having an affair with a female employee, who in turn was taking advantage of the company. The young man heard about this in an office gathering and quickly passed it on to his 'best friend' who handled communication. Now this latter person had a strained relationship with the Operations Head, and was seeking an opportunity to settle the score. The young man gave him just the opportunity. Within an hour, the news spread like wildfire across the company and even outside the company—you can imagine what happened after that. The King called for an emergency meeting and ordered a probe. After many days, it was proved that the news was spread by the young man and his 'friend'. And they never lived happily ever after.

How does it matter to you if someone is getting a promotion or a transfer? How does it matter to you if someone got a bashing from his boss? How does it matter to you if someone is having an extramarital affair? Frankly, none of these should bother you. You must develop the maturity to stay away from such gossip. You are here to work and deliver results. You must concentrate on your career, rather than spread rumours about what is happening around you.

Office gossip is always great to pass the time, but it does not help your career. To me, it's a sheer waste of time. Watch out for gossipmongers. It's difficult to stay away from them completely, since you are a normal human being, but be extremely careful of how to handle them.

Take a step back and talk to yourself. How can these rumours, even if they are true, help your career? You have limited time in a day; you have to decide how to utilize it. Is it not better to concentrate on your work in the little time available rather than pay attention to the grapevine?

You are in the corporate jungle now. You are short on time. Believe me, time passes so quickly that even before you realize it, your career will be over! You have so much to achieve and such little time. If you really can't stay without tittle-tattle, choose a different place to gossip, away from your workplace. You have friends, you have family. But please, the office is not the place for gossip. Don't waste your precious years in believing or spreading hearsay. No one trusts those who create or spread gossip. People doubt their integrity.

This is exactly what happened to the young man in the story. He was sucked into the rumour mill and happened to speak to his 'friend', who was just waiting for an opportunity to act against the Operations Head. In the process, the young man jeopardized his own dream career.

Don't play politics at work

There is nothing politically right that is morally wrong.— Daniel O'Connell

Once upon a time, there was a King, the CEO of a company, undergoing a rough patch. The board of directors took a hard call and decided to overhaul the entire top management; they believed that those people were responsible for the company's downfall. In the process, the company also appointed the King as the new head of the business.

After a few years, the company turned around. It started growing again, making profits and regaining market share. Everybody got their share of appreciation, especially the sales head, since the board felt that he was the pivot for the turnaround. The King was so pleased with it that he personally recommended a promotion and hefty salary increase for the sales head.

The excessive praise spoilt the sales head. He soon began to dream of becoming the next King. He calculated and realized that he needed to wait out a few more years before being considered for that position. But the sales head was not ready to wait. In his mind, he was ready to take up the big leap, so he planned to oust the King.

Ironically, the King trusted the sales head implicitly and discussed future strategies with him. The King valued his opinion the most. The sales head knew one of the directors on the board from an earlier association. Through him, over next few months, he started building up relationships with the other board members. Before any board meeting, the sales head would informally share company strategy with the directors. Thus, before the meeting, the directors would already know what the King was going to share.

The King was unaware of this game, but the board started to believe that the sales head was the man behind the company's vision, while the King was just a messenger. They soon started to doubt the King's ability, and, within a few months, decided to appoint the sales head as the new King.

The new King ruled the company for a year, working on the strategy laid down by the earlier King. He had nothing of his own to contribute to the business. After a year, the company's performance started going down again. The board was surprised not to find any new plan being discussed by the new King, and soon realized that sacking the earlier King was a huge mistake. History was repeated; the new King was asked to vacate the throne, and the old King was brought back to run the show. And the new King never lived happily ever after.

We might choose not to believe it, but office politics exists in all companies. It is natural. The journey to the top is not easy. The corporate pyramid suggests that everybody will not reach the top, and so, competition creeps in. Some people will always look for an easy route, and find it easier to bypass others by playing politics. They are fools, for sure.

Though you will be within the ambit of office politics, you must keep away from it. It's difficult but doable. It's a dirty game played by some dirty-minded people. You need to be careful. You need to keep your mind open and observe what's happening around you. You should not be prey to it. All you need to do is learn to detect early warning signals and try to stay untouched by such acts motivated by vested interests.

In every organization, there are some people clearly known to be political, and some who steer clear of the political rigmarole. Both kinds do well in their careers. The difference is that the people who play politics are never at peace. They have to keep thinking about their next move.

You are here to work, so talk about work. Avoid discussing people. Appreciate people rather than criticize them. No one is perfect. Never talk about a person when he or she is not around; the other person has every right to know your opinion firsthand, not through a distorted story.

Most people who play politics lack confidence in themselves. I'm sure you won't—you are here because you are confident. It is not worth trying to play politics even for a day. You will have more foes than friends. It may work in the short run, but life is a great leveller. It will catch up with you in the long run. You need well-wishers at work, you need your colleagues to help you move ahead. Negative thoughts and a political mind will never fetch you those so don't waste your precious years by playing politics!

Avoid senseless humour

Some people are commended for a giddy kind of good humour, which is no more a virtue than drunkenness.—Alexander Pope

Once upon a time, there was a young man known for his quick wit. He was probably the funniest guy in the college and was called Laughter Express. He was the most popular member of his class, especially among girls. People loved his presence; without him the college canteen was a boring place. He was invited to all the parties for his entertainment value. He cracked all kind of jokes. He cherished his popularity. The habit stayed with him even when he joined the corporate world. In fact, very soon, he became popular among his peers for his amazing sense of humour.

One day, at an office party, this young man was in full swing. A large group of people was thronging him, listening to him. There was a young lady in the group, also enjoying his jokes. In one of his jokes, this young man took that lady name as an example. It was about an extramarital affair between a young lady and the King, her boss.

For once, after the young man delivered the punchline, no one laughed. There was complete silence. People found that joke to be out of place, quite inappropriate. The young lady left the place in a huff. The young man could not understand why and decided to ignore it. He never knew that this young lady truly had an affair with the King!

The next day, the young lady lodged a complaint against the young man, accusing him of spreading rumours about her. The complaint took an ugly turn and went into an inquiry. Luckily, his boss stood up for him and requested the King not to take tough action. He counselled the young man to be careful. The matter was settled when the young man agreed to walk up to the young lady and apologize. He didn't like the entire episode, however, and left the job after some time. Till then, he never lived happily in that organization.

There is nothing wrong in being the Laughter Express, especially when, as a new entrant, you find the corporate world to be suffocating. You may find enough serious-faced people all around. If you can make people smile, they will enjoy your company in the corporate world, but you need to be extremely careful. There is a difference between college days and the corporate life. A joke appropriate in a college canteen may be quite out of place in the corporate office. You need to evaluate every word you speak.

Every corporate is different; the cultures are diverse. You need to be completely aware of the culture before you take any step. For instance, the culture in a film production company would be completely different from that in a company that sells molasses. Even the culture in a manufacturing location will differ from the head office of the same company.

Don't try too hard to gain popularity. Be who you are, but tweak yourself to fit into this new culture. Never adopt a style that is not natural to you. In the jungle, you need to be cautious all the time. You must be acutely aware of the time, the place and what you utter. Office pranks are fine, but choose the audience and timing carefully.

The young man, intent on entertaining his colleagues, did not pay attention to the selection of his jokes or characters; he did not try and pay heed to others' sentiments. Such a wrong move can cost a person heavily, and a lost reputation may take years to restore. The sooner we learn this, the easier will be our journey through the jungle.

Never lose control of yourself

Not to have control over the senses is like sailing in a rudderless ship, bound to break to pieces on coming in contact with the very first rock.—Mahatma Gandhi

Once upon a time, there was a company where Family Day was the most awaited corporate gathering. It was a mandatory occasion for all employees, and all the directors, promoters and their families attended it. The company also celebrated the day as an annual award-giving day for employees. No one wanted to miss this occasion; it was a good time to connect with people. It was a great occasion to meet and greet, reunite and unwind.

The King, the CEO of the company, and his Queen ensured that they spend adequate time with each employee and his family. The King personally ensured that every arrangement was perfect, so that his employees had a really good time. He did not want to cut corners.

This time, there was a young lady who had joined the company two years ago. She had missed the previous year's party due to an illness and was very excited to attend her first corporate annual party. This year's party was even more special, as she had been nominated for the Best Young Manager award.

After receiving the award, the young lady joined her group of friends at the bar. At their request, she took a drink, but decided she would leave the party as soon as she finished it. In a while, the discussion became interesting and she forget her promise. In any case, she was quite elated, as everyone passing by was congratulating her. She felt special, she felt proud.

Soon, the dance floor was opened and groups of people took to the floor. The young lady was also pulled in. She resisted, since she wanted to leave, but no one would let her. After all, it was *her* day! Despite her resistance, her friends kept on serving her drinks. Soon, she felt quite high and a bit out of control. She left the dance floor to sit in a corner and just enjoy her drink and watch the crowd, but her friends pulled her back to the bar. It was the time for vodka shots.

In a while, the young lady saw the King dancing too. She had always admired him. In fact, she had developed an infatuation for him. She pulled the King off the dance floor and said, 'Sir, can I have a drink with you please? It will be an honour for me.'

'I don't think you should drink any more,' replied the King.

'Stop this lecture, sir . . . As the best employee of the year, I demand a drink with you!'

The King realized that the young lady was not in her senses, so he accompanied her to the bar to avoid an ugly scene. As the bartender poured the drinks, she said, 'I truly admire you, sir. I really want to be like you one day.'

'Thanks a lot,' said the King, 'Let us have a quick drink; I have to go back on stage.'

'Come on, sir, we don't get a chance to interact like this every day!' replied the young lady.

The King looked at her, surprised. She then moved close to him and whispered in his ear, 'Can I have a close dance with you? I know your wife is not around now.'

The King smiled and said, 'Thank you, another day perhaps. I need to leave now . . .' He left the bar quickly, requesting the HR director to escort her away from the party.

The King did not take any action against the young lady; he believed that the incident was a one-off aberration. But, when the young lady regained her senses, she realized her mistake. It was difficult for her to face the King. She definitely did not live happily for a long time after that.

A corporate party is not a college fest or a friend's bash where you can drink till the wee hours, speak your heart out, think at every hour that the night was still young and finally stay back and sleep on the floor! I'm sure it has happened to all of us. It starts with 'just one drink' and ends with 'one for the road', 'one for the elevator', 'one for old times' and so on . . . And then, the next day you get up with a massive headache, wondering: 'Oh crap! How did I reach home last night? Who dropped me? How did I drive my bike? What things did I say? Hope I didn't talk rubbish! Was anyone laughing at me? No more drinking and driving,' and so on, till you finally assure yourself and say, 'Anyway, who cares? All of us were drunk . . . No one will remember anything!' And you promise yourself, 'No more nonsense. Next time, just one drink!' Right?

Please remember that you have grown up, which is why you are now in a corporate. Want to drink? Please drink, but drink responsibly. That is what any sensible corporate honcho does. No one will now be interested in all the stories you made up when you were drunk in college!

A corporate life is all about showing that you are always in control; you are not expected to lose control even for a moment. If you wish to express your mind freely, please go back to your friends and enjoy, but never do so—not once—in a corporate party. Always stay in control in an office gathering.

Avoid having an affair at work

If you plough the land you dwell, where will you have your home?—Popular saying

Once upon a time, there was a young man who was transferred to a factory to take over as the finance head. He felt lucky to get this job quite early in his career. In the previous three years at this company, his growth had been astounding. Many eyebrows were raised when he was offered this new designation, but the rock-solid reputation he had built silenced his critics.

In the plant, he met a young lady from the HR department. She helped him settle down at his new job. She made the extra effort to take him around to select a house, open bank accounts and so on. After checking out many apartments, the young man finally selected an apartment in the housing complex where this young lady lived.

Now, this lady was married to a sailor, who used to be away at sea for months. She lived in the apartment with her four-year-old daughter. Soon the young lady and the young man became good friends. Being a bachelor, he often visited her for dinner. She enjoyed his company, as it kept her from getting bored. After a while, they decided to commute to office in one car to save money. Even on the weekends, they were found together at malls or cinema halls. People started to talk about their relationship. The young man was soon termed her 'second husband'.

They heard it too, but didn't bother. The young man believed that he was unimpeachable due to all the smart work he put in and his impeccable track record. He was wrong. The news soon reached the head office, and they were charged for having an affair. The company discouraged office romances and both of them were sent a show-cause notice. They were called to the head office to explain why no action should be taken against them for violating office ethics and having an affair with a colleague. The matter was finally referred to a code of conduct committee, which found them guilty and stopped their increments for two years.

The young man felt extremely humiliated. He spoke to his seniors, who had always supported him in his career. He explained to them that it was just a friendship—nothing besides—and that it didn't affect his work in the least. But no one was in the mood to listen to him. For them, violation of ethics outweighed efficiency.

The young man resigned the next month. The news reached the young lady's husband as well, and, in a few years, their bitter marriage ended in a divorce. Neither of them lived happily ever after.

Having a friend of the opposite sex in office is normal. No one can object to it, as long as the two of you are good friends and maintain a visible distance. You need to be cautious and manage perceptions carefully. There are many instances where people have got married after meeting each other in an office. There are also many instances where people got divorced, and remarried, after meeting each other in an office. The examples are diverse. First of all, check out the rules and decide for yourself. While some offices allow you to continue your employment even after marrying a colleague, and may even appreciate your step since they might believe that it is a tool for talent retention, others may completely discourage it and insist that one of you leaves.

However, it is certain that no corporate would appreciate an adulterous affair! You are there to make a career. You are paid to work for the company, not to have an affair. You might think that it is a matter of your personal life, but the company may believe that an affair would affect your performance. Many might feel that it spoils the corporate atmosphere. It is always better to be safe than sorry. Why should you waste your formative years on something the company may not appreciate?

The young man in the story probably did not have an affair with the young lady. And this fact was probably quite clear in his mind. But the corporate world perceived it differently and he had to pay the price. Similarly, for the young lady, she not only lost her reputation but also landed into personal jeopardy. You can decide for yourself. The earlier you decide, the better it is for your career.

Learn how to behave with the opposite sex

Behaviour is a mirror in which everyone displays his own image.—Johann Wolfgang von Goethe

Once upon a time, there was a young man and a young lady who worked in the same office. The young man was the senior by designation. Though the young lady did not report to him, they needed to meet for a few hours every day. However, she didn't like the way he interacted with her. In fact, she didn't want to communicate with him at all, but had no option.

The young man had a habit of making uncalled-for comments and indirect remarks about her appearance and clothes. The young lady tolerated this for some time. The young man gained confidence and started looking for occasions to pat her on the back, shake her hand, touch her . . . Being a woman, she intuitively understood his intention. Yet, in the beginning, she didn't say anything to him.

The young man's advances became more intense. He started sending regular emails with implicit sexual propositions. She started to avoid him, restricting her conversation strictly to work. He never understood that she did not like his overtures. He became even bolder. One evening, he asked her to join him for a cup of coffee at the cafe next door. The young lady did not refuse.

As they spoke, the young man openly appreciated her beautiful figure. She kept quiet, and did not react. Sensing his opportunity, just before dropping her off, he said, 'I know you like me . . . Same here.'

The young lady was taken aback. She just wanted to get home quickly.

He said, 'I know the meaning of your silence. I'm a grown-up man. There is no one at home today. My wife will return only tomorrow. Let's have coffee at my place?'

The young lady nearly broke down. Controlling herself, she said firmly, 'Drop me home now.'

The young man kept pleading but she refused to accompany him. In some time, he reluctantly dropped her home.

The young lady was somewhat of an introvert. She didn't have too many friends in the office and seldom spoke to people outside her work. However, bothered by the incident, she shared it with a colleague who worked in the young man's department. The other lady heard her out and said, 'So I'm not alone.'

She then revealed that the young man was harassing her as well. She said, 'I thought he was genuinely in love with me. He even proposed to divorce his wife to get married to me. Now I know his real character! This is his nature. I think we deserve better people around us in office. The time has come to teach him the right lesson.'

The two ladies lodged a complaint with the King, the HR head. An investigation was conducted, and, in a few weeks, the young man was asked to resign. The news spread to other organizations as well, and it became extremely difficult for the young man to find another job. A bright career was destroyed and he never lived happily ever after.

Some behaviour is never acceptable in the corporate world. You need to be careful, especially when dealing with the opposite sex. Corporates always have strict policies on sexual harassment and deal with it in a tough manner.

In college, touching each other while talking, sending funny e-mails or jokes may be acceptable, because you are among friends. These things are part of your growing up. But now that you are grown-ups, you are supposed to behave in a way that this jungle expects and accepts. A simple slip may cost you dearly. In many cases, you might end up losing your job.

The first objective is to know the office policy well and follow it all the time. We have joined this corporate world to work hard and to be successful in our careers. That should be our only objective. We should be alert at every moment that we don't violate company policy.

Please remember, in the case of such complaints, it is usually your word against the other person's. Even if you have ample proof of your being in the right, you may still lose your reputation.

Till it was all going smooth, the young man did not realize what he was headed for. He was playing around with the young ladies in his office and never expected to get exposed. He considered this lady to be an easy target, thinking she would never share the matter with anyone else. Just one wrong move nailed him down in no time. Throughout his life, the young man had to live with the stigma of getting sacked for sexual harassment.

Do you want to end your budding career like that? I'm sure not. So, be very careful!

Never disagree after you agree

The people to fear are not those who disagree with you, but those who disagree with you and are too cowardly to let you know.—Napoleon Bonaparte

Once upon a time, there was a King who was the CEO of a company. Those days, commodity prices were on an upswing, and the company's profitability was under severe pressure. The King requested his team for a price increase to make up for the additional costs. He communicated his intention in different forums, but no action was taken for nearly two months. The King was surprised, for he had never earlier faced a situation like that. All his discussions with the functional heads concluded positively and each assured him individually that a price increase would be affected. However, when he cross-checked, he realized that nothing had moved, as some functional heads decided to ignore his request. No price increase was communicated to the market.

He called his Minister, the COO, and asked for the reason. The Minister informed him that the sales and finance heads were not in favour of the price increase, as they feared it would cause a volume drop resulting in an overall profit drop.

The King exclaimed, 'But they agreed with me in my office!'

Then he thought for a while and requested the Minister to organize a quick meeting with all the leaders. Soon, the leadership team converged on the board room. The King entered and locked the door. The leaders were surprised at his unusual action.

The King sat down on his throne and said, 'Sorry for this short notice and thanks for being here. I'm here to discuss the price increase about which you had agreed with me earlier, but have not taken any action to date. You alone know the reason for your inaction. Now, you all know that we have cost challenges and I feel that we must take our prices up. However, I don't force any action. We will do whatever is right for the company.'

He paused and said, 'I have locked the door as I want us to come to a consensus, whatever it may be. We will discuss till we come to a conclusion and no one goes out till we all agree to one decision. We can argue, fight, discuss. We might decide for or against the price hike but we won't leave the room till we agree. I would like to exit this room with one and only one decision. Hope I have your support.'

The leaders understood the message. The King smiled and said, 'Don't worry, I've arranged for food as well. I won't keep you starving!'

The meeting lasted for almost twelve hours. Everybody argued passionately. Finally, they decided not to increase the prices. Satisfied with the process, the King smiled and said, 'Thank you, folks, for such a passionate discussion. We now have a decision and I am happy that it is our collective decision. A piece of advice to you all—never disagree after you agree. That's not what I expect from my professional managers. We should put across all our arguments before a decision is taken, but once agreed it should be "our" decision.'

The finance and the sales heads also got the message and

decided to change their behaviour. And they lived happily ever after.

What I've told in the story is not easy to follow. We want all decisions to turn out the way we think is right. In reality, though, the decisions taken by a team can differ from what you may have proposed. Even so, we need to align our minds to go ahead and implement a collective decision. A corporate cannot be run with people driving towards different directions.

Take, for instance, a project. There will be a leader or a group of people leading the project and team members supporting them. There will be discussions, there will be arguments, there will be differences in opinion. That is the way any team works. In that confusion, every member of the team is expected to contribute not only by working for the project but also by participating in the decision-making. Collective consensus is always better than an individual decision.

Some companies have a culture that allows intense discussions; some companies dislike argument and confrontation; some encourage peaceful deliberation. That is the way different companies operate. Some meetings can take hours to build consensus; some may take barely a few moments to agree on the next steps. Those are the processes, and you have every right to argue till you are satisfied but then, once a decision is taken and its logic has been provided, you must respect it. You must become part of that decision.

No company likes people to come out of a meeting and

then declare to the whole world that they don't agree on a decision taken in the meeting. That's unprofessional, a strict no-no. It should always be discouraged. It not only creates bad blood, but, if it becomes an attitude, it will destroy trust in the team. It is a waste of time. It is neither good for the organization nor for the individual. The sooner you learn this, the better it is for you in your careers.

Never become a yes-man

Learn to say 'no' to the good, so you can say 'yes' to the best.
—John C. Maxwell

Once upon a time, there was a young man who worked in the corporate strategy department of a large corporation. He reported to a lady, who headed the strategy department. In a short time, the young man had established himself so well in the system that without him the young lady felt crippled. The young man respected his boss for her sharp business acumen and foresight. The only trait he disliked is her was that she changed her stance quite frequently. Often they agreed on a strategy after debating for hours, but she changed her position in a blink when the King, the CEO, commented otherwise! The young man now knew that though she was bright, if the King countered her, she would give way and agree to even the most insipid logic of the King.

Interestingly, whenever the young man displayed his dissent after such a letdown, the lady would find some logic to justify her action. The young man hated those moments. He felt cheated that all his hard work, all his analytical acrobatics, all his late nights went down the drain in no time!

In the month of September, the strategy department was helping the management finalize the numbers for the next year. The next meeting was to decide on the next year's capital budget. The lady had requested the young man to present to the approving committee on her behalf. Before the meeting, they agreed on the presentation strategy. It was an important meeting—they needed the capital but they also knew that the management was risk-averse and it was not going to be easy to get the capital sanctioned. They needed the capital, as the market was growing, the competition was putting up new facilities and they could not afford to run out of capacity. They were both convinced of this.

On this day, since he was presenting the case himself to the leadership team, the young man decided to push his conviction. He prepared for several hours. It was a great opportunity to showcase his talent to the King. The meeting started well, with the young man moving slide by slide to explain why the company needed capital. From the reactions of those present, the young man gained confidence. From their body language, he could see that the people were listening to him and the acceptance level was high. At the end of his presentation, the lady gestured to him that he had done well, boosting his confidence further. Then, the leadership team put down its view and asked for a few clarifications. The young man answered each query convincingly.

The meeting was nearly over, when the King said, 'Young man, I liked your presentation. You have a logical point, but I think we should wait. We should not invest now. I don't want to take a risk. Let's see what the competition does. I want them to move first.'

'But, your highness . . .'

The King stopped the young man and said, 'I told you that I liked what you said, but I would still wait and watch.'

'But sir, I'm convinced, as are the other members here. If you wish, I can work on the details further and meet you again with another approach. I'm confident that you will change your mind. Sir, we need investment and we need it now.'

'No young man, I'm not here to gamble. I always play safe, and will continue to do so. I hope I am communicating well to you.'

The young man looked to his boss for support. But, as usual, she said to the King, 'Your highness, I think you are right. I'm also not convinced by what was presented! I think we need to rework the strategy. Let us look at an approach without capital investment.'

'But ma'am, we worked on this together,' exclaimed the young man, rather brusquely.

The lady ignored his comment and said, 'Don't worry. I will help you this time. We have some ground to cover.'

'But ma'am, you just gestured to me that I did well. Every word that I uttered today was agreed to by you.' Only after he blurted this out did the young man realize that his comment was out of place. The room suddenly was completely in silence and then everyone started to giggle.

The King said, 'I was testing your conviction. I'm glad we have people like you in our company who can look ahead. You don't need to prepare any more slides. I was convinced the moment you finished your presentation. We must go ahead. Good job, young man!'

He then looked at the lady and said, 'You have bright people in your team, you must take care of them.' Her jaw dropped, and all the others got the King's message loud and clear.

The King left shortly, after sanctioning the young man's investment proposal. And the lady never lived happily ever after.

Becoming a yes-man to seniors is the easiest thing to do. You may feel that it is the simplest way to the top. You will be wrong. It may help in the short term but, in the long term, this one trait can kill a person as a professional.

When you start your career, your confidence level is probably at the peak. You are ready to take on the world. Then you meet many leaders and notice that most of them are different from each other. Invariably, some of them will be the yes-man type. Please do not idolize them.

Please be aware of the fact that you have an independent mind and views. Please do not echo what your boss says. If you follow that route, you will soon have nothing to contribute to the business. In some years, you will lose respect in the organization and also the confidence for challenging a situation. You are paid to contribute to the business, not to say yes to the man who is responsible for your appraisal or increment.

It isn't always the fault of the young person like you. Several bosses would like their subordinates to agree with them all the time; in fact, there are only a few who like being challenged. We must choose the right way and not fall into this trap to please our supervisor. There's nothing wrong in becoming the boss's favourite, but that should happen through our efforts and our conviction. We have joined a corporation to grow ourselves and to add value to the business, not to become popular with the boss. Bosses will come and go but, as individuals, we must do what is right for the company and for ourselves.

The young man's situation is not unique. Many people face such dilemmas. I'm sure that, after the meeting, he did not have a smooth run with the lady. He probably paid for it in the short run, but who cares? For his life and career, he followed the right path. He did what was right for the organization as well as for him. And he learnt it early in his career.

Avoid following an individual

The foot feels the foot when it feels the ground.—Ernest Wood

Once upon a time, there was a young man who joined the company as a management trainee. The King, the CFO of the company, was looking for a good data analyst. He wanted to know the real problem in the company and this young man's job was to provide him intelligent analysis.

The young man had an analytical bent of mind and he loved his job. He helped the King with smart analyses, which equipped the King to ask the right questions in any interaction. The King loved him as well and soon became completely dependent on this young man. The young man too enjoyed his elevated status; after all, he was the only person from his batch of management trainees who moved with the King all the time. His batchmates envied him. Though he enjoyed his position, he didn't let his success go to his head and kept delivering excellent results day after day.

After about a year, the King left the job to join another company. The young man felt disheartened. The King too was nervous, as he depended on the young man too much. They reached an agreement. The young man would support the King in his off-time and over weekends. After a few months, once the King established himself in his new assignment, the young man would join him at a much higher salary than in the current company. He worked extra to support the King and, in a few months, the King too kept his promise of offering him a job. The young man moved ahead of his batchmates, joining the King at almost double his starting salary. His life became even better.

Unfortunately, in the new company, the young man found it extremely difficult to settle in. People took his ideas with a pinch of salt. He was known as 'the King's man'. He tried his best to build a rapport with his new colleagues, but the people felt he could not be taken into confidence as he would pass information on to the King. People kept their distance from him.

After a while, the young man decided not to bother—after all, he was truly the King's man, much more privileged than the others. But then, something happened. The young man's new company was taken over by another company, and, as a matter of policy, they had to appoint a new CFO. Hence, one fine day, the King was asked to leave the organization. Life without the King became miserable for the young man. He lost all his power, since the new management started to ignore him. He tried his best to mend certain relationships, but it was too late. Soon he had to quit. For a long time, till he found another job, he never lived happily.

This is the worst thing that can happen to you—to be marked as your boss's man. You lose your identity as an individual. Your brilliance or your contribution to the company does not matter any more. What matters to the world is that you are 'tagged'. This happened to the young man. He liked and respected his boss, who reciprocated by giving him a nice break. But he was soon perceived to be a non-entity without his boss.

That is absolutely undesirable. Yet, it can happen to anyone—knowingly or unknowingly. When the young man left his job to follow the King, he did so since he had a comfort factor working with the King and was being paid much more than others. He knew that the King recognized his calibre and hence he had an assured chance to succeed in the new company.

There is nothing wrong in what the young man did. He sensed the opportunity and grabbed it. Many people do that—it is human nature. We all like our success and would like to achieve it in a safe zone. We would also like to spend time with a person whom we love or respect. Where the young man failed was that he could not manage his perception and relationship with the world beyond the King. He allowed himself to be tagged as the King's man. So when the King landed in trouble, the young man too became a victim for no fault of his.

I'm not suggesting that you should never join a company where your former boss works. I'm suggesting that you must tread carefully. There is a risk attached to every action you take so try to recognize the risk and be ready to mitigate it proactively before you go ahead.

Several people have done well by following an individual; you can be the next. There are also plenty of young men and women who have ruined their careers by following an individual. Please ensure that you are not the next!

***

The day ended. It was time to pack up. Mr Chatterjee asked, 'We now need to summarize what we discussed during the day in a few words . . . What should we say?'

I raised my hand and said, 'Fabulous!'

Mr Chatterjee laughed and said, 'I was not fishing for compliments. Let us elaborate . . . Anyone else?'

Another member of the group said, 'We learnt to walk through the jungle. We learnt the rules of the jungle. We learnt the dos and the don'ts.'

'That's right, but what did we learn?' reiterated Mr Chatterjee.

Another member said, 'We learnt the importance of understanding what is expected of us and then of managing those expectations. Honouring and delivering commitments every time are critical.'

I added, 'We also learnt the importance of being practical about learning from the job. There is nothing wrong in saying: "I am a student; teach me." Even after many years of work experience, we have enough left to learn.'

Another member said, 'This reminds me of having the courage to accept my mistakes.'

'We should also appreciate that no one wants us to throw problems at them without suggesting solutions. Let us think of a possible solution before posing a problem to others since we will probably know how best to resolve issues in our purview,' said another.

'We spoke about certain basic rules of the corporate world, which may be different from the norms of our college lives. We need to conduct ourselves in a certain manner and follow certain rules and etiquette that are acceptable in this new world,' said yet another member.

'Above all, we learnt that we should always work in a team. If our team is successful, we will succeed too.' I said.

'And don't forget to achieve quick wins; they will boost your confidence,' said Mr Chatterjee.

'We also learnt about a few things that we must avoid all the time,' I said.

'Unfortunately, as I said earlier, those were the very

things that I too was looking forward to when I took up my first job,' said Mr Chatterjee.

We all laughed.

'No, I'm serious. Someone told me that I must stay tuned to what is happening around me, so I thought office gossip is important. I watched how my first boss played politics at work, how he got his own boss sacked through a wrong allegation of sexual harassment and quickly took over the job himself. I saw him getting drunk at office parties and blurting out certain facts, which otherwise he probably wouldn't have. He still succeeded.

'I saw leaders criticizing certain decisions despite being party to them; I have even seen people changing sides at the behest of their bosses. I used to adore them, thinking that was the right way to the top. But then one day I spoke to myself and decided not to follow the wrong leaders. After many years, when I look back now, I realize that I am here today because I decided not to follow the wrong people and take the wrong path. Interestingly, most of those leaders have fallen by the way,' said Mr Chatterjee, though humbly.

We nodded. My respect for Mr Chatterjee escalated.

It was time to go home. I waited for a long walk again.

SECTION 3

SURVIVING IN THE JUNGLE

We knew it was the second last session with Mr Chatterjee. We all wanted to glean whatever more we could from a person who had already become a larger-than-life character for us. Mr Chatterjee said, 'Today we will speak about certain traits we must master. This is clearly derived from my experience and my opinion on what we must possess as professionals. During my years in the corporate world, I watched many people closely. I realized that each successful person is different, and has a unique work style. Yet, they share some traits, some hallmarks of success. Today I am going to share those common characteristics.'

Ask the right question

The important thing is not to stop questioning. Curiosity has its own reason for existing.—Albert Einstein

Once upon a time, there was a Minister, the CFO of a multinational. A successful man, with many years of experience in the same company, he believed that he knew everything. He was convinced that he was the most informed individual around. In meetings, he did not expect to be questioned. Indeed, whatever he said was accepted by other members as the truth. In fact, no one ever dared to ask him any question.

One day, a young man joined the company as executive assistant to the CEO. He was a very intelligent young man with a few years of experience. His job involved a lot of interaction with the learned Minister.

Now, this young man was a new-age professional; he wanted to know everything behind the numbers. So, he asked the Minister a lot of questions. The Minister did not like his approach, and, being the most powerful man after the King, he complained that the young man doubted his knowledge and ability. The King called the Minister and the young man for a discussion and heard them out.

The King said to the young man, 'The Minister has many years of experience, while you have only a few. You also know that he does not like to be questioned. Are you not afraid that you are risking your career by asking him all sorts of questions?'

'No, your highness,' answered the young man fearlessly.

'But why?' asked the surprised King. The Minister too waited for an answer.

'It is simple, your highness. There are two reasons. First, what I ask is what I need to know for my job. I think I have every right to know it. Hence I am not scared.'

'And what is the other reason?' asked the Minister. The young man's confidence infuriated him.

'The second reason is that I always ask myself: "Should I?" before asking any question. If I get a positive response from my inner self, I know that what I'm asking is needed for the business.'

The King let the young man go. He looked at the Minister and said, 'I'm impressed with this young man. It is a lesson for me as well. Life has changed, Mr Minister. Gone are those days where we were beyond questioning. In today's corporate world, everybody has the right to know since the decisions we take affect people's lives. I urge you to change your style of working, be more open and cooperate with these new-age professionals.'

The Minister left the meeting dismayed, realizing that he also needed to change, even at his advanced age.

And the young man lived happily ever after.

You have every right to ask the right question. You have every right to get the information that matters to your job. You are neither probing for any personal detail, nor asking for something unrelated to the business. So, why should you shy away from asking?

We all underestimate the power of asking questions. Most of us are raised in situations where asking questions is a taboo; we are meant to follow instructions. Often, the correct way is indicated to us, but we are not allowed to explore why it is the correct way!

But the world is changing fast. We are moving into a new-age education system, a much more open culture. People are encouraged to ask what they want to know. So why not change ourselves to suit the new requirement? Till the time you ask a question, you are listening. You are absorbing a discussion and talking to yourselves silently. The moment you open your mouths and ask a question, people around you also get involved. So, you need to be careful and ask what needs to be asked; after all, you do expect someone to answer. It involves time, energy and effort from either side. It consumes resources, which consume money. You need to be relevant and think carefully before asking questions.

I liked what the young man did in the story. Before asking a question, you should also ask yourselves: 'Should I?' If you get a positive response from your inner selves, go ahead. But, interestingly, the moment you double-check with yourselves, many questions will get answered without even being asked.

The fact is that we all know we must ask the right questions, but it is often difficult to define the right question. The difference between the right and the not-so-right question emerges when you check with yourselves. It is not easy to master the art but, if we start early, you will soon succeed.

Always be prepared

The way to secure peace is to be prepared for the war.
—Benjamin Franklin

Once upon a time, there was a young man who joined a start-up venture. He was known to be a start-up specialist and the King, the owner of the company, hand-picked him to set up processes for his organization. Initially, the young man was reluctant to leave his job in a larger corporation but then he sensed the opportunity—and the accompanying money, position and power—and acceded to the King's request. He knew that, with the King's support, he would be able to implement any process that he wanted to take the company forward, thus ensuring success for himself and the King.

Within two months of his joining the company, the King requested him to put forth his initial observations and recommendations to the leadership team. The King thought it would be a good opportunity to showcase the kind of new processes he wanted this young man to operationalize. For the young man, it was his first opportunity to talk to the leadership team. The King was very excited about the meeting as well, since he was expecting great results to come out of it. The meeting began, the young man presented the proposed changes. The team listened to him for a while . . . But then, some members reacted.

The sales head said, 'I'm not convinced with your presentation. I'm not clear . . . What is going to change?'

The finance head nodded: 'I completely agree with the sales head. You are just projecting things nicely. These slides look great but I don't think they are workable solutions. They are too theoretical, not applicable to our industry.'

The HR head replied, 'I agree that those are some lovely intentions. They may have worked in your earlier company but they are not suitable for us.'

The young man responded, 'I have earned my living through these processes for many years. They work.'

'But what is there for us in them? Why should we change

our existing processes that work well?' asked the finance head.

'I don't care. I'm not here to explain. We need to follow these new processes.'

'But why?' asked the HR head.

The young man fumbled, he had no answer. He kept repeating that they should adapt the new processes since he thought those were the right processes. He had no sound logic to support his statements. The leadership team refused to agree to his recommendations. The discussion turned into a fight and the King had to intervene when the sales head said sarcastically, 'Stealing with pride is good, but you should do it intelligently. The next time, at least change the slide background—it shows the logo of your earlier company!'

The group burst into laughter.

The young man said arrogantly, 'You all have blocked minds. That is why the company has not taken off even after being in operation for two years. I'm convinced that this is the only way we can take this company forward . . .'

The King stepped in and said, 'I think we need to reconvene. This meeting is not going anywhere.'

In a while, he met the young man in his office and asked, 'Do you realize why you failed today? You failed because you were not prepared. You took those people for granted.'

'But I know the processes well! They ganged up and refused to let me explain,' replied the young man.

'It doesn't matter. Even if you know the processes well, you should have prepared yourself to suit today's need. I found you clearly underprepared for today's discussion. You have missed a golden opportunity.' The King thought for a while and said, 'Let's try again. I'll call another meeting soon.'

The young man learnt his lesson and prepared himself well to present his recommendations to the team with more facts and figures. In the next meeting, he was on top of things, choosing every word carefully and answering every query well. The leadership team agreed to his recommendations with minor tweaks.

The young man lived happily ever after.

Preparation before any interaction is the key to success. Along with preparation, the trait that can guarantee the successful outcome of an interaction is our decision to be present. Being present does not mean physical presence alone but mental presence too. In the corporate world, every interaction—be it formal or informal—is important. Any interaction will involve your peers, juniors, seniors or outsiders. They are all human and watching you at every moment. To win them over, you should be willing to be present in every moment.

You should not attend a meeting just because someone invited you. You should be there because you have chosen to be there, to add value. If you are mentally absent, you cannot add value to any interaction. If you are carving out time from your own life to attend a meeting, justify your presence. You are in a meeting because someone thought you could add value to the process—so you have no right to be unprepared. Preparation makes us confident. It gives us the ability to add value to a process, to take the process forward. People who attend meetings without preparation are detrimental to the business. Even the most boring meeting should find you in a positive frame of mind. Positive energy spreads and your energy may make a meeting fruitful.

Often, seniors, peers, even juniors will ask you unpleasant questions. These questions can really catch you off guard. At times, you may take them personally and react badly. Each and every word you say is important, each and every gesture is vital. You will be in control only when you decide to be mentally present and amply prepared. A well-aware, well-prepared mind will help you tackle any situation better. Take every moment seriously. Always think of a moment when you suddenly have the opportunity to travel with your CEO in a lift for the next two-three minutes. As a CEO, he can ask you any question relating to your job and to avoid a career-limiting moment, you need to convey your thoughts with enough clarity and conviction (popularly what people term as the 'elevator speech').

Thus, be prepared and be present all the time, from the day you enter the jungle.

Be assertive

To know oneself, one should assert oneself.—Albert Camus

Once upon a time, a young man joined an organization. He was fresh out of college and bright enough to impress everyone in a short time. He was soon appreciated for his performance and for his ability to get things done. He was also loved by his colleagues for his nice behaviour and positive attitude. He started growing swiftly in the organization and became a department head within a few years. By virtue of this position, he became the youngest member of the leadership team. This was a big job for the young man; he started reporting directly to the King, the CEO.

Being a departmental head, he was expected to do what his boss used to do till a few months ago—attend leadership meetings, run the department, delegate jobs, get people to agree to his views, take decisions, manage people's careers and so on. In simple words, from a purely executive job, where he was used to little decision-making and more of following instructions, he suddenly graduated to a job that required managing people.

The sudden leap made the young man a bit nervous as he knew that he was not mentally prepared for this big job. His behaviour changed within months of this jump. To show his supremacy, he soon picked conflicts with his peers and became abrasive towards his subordinates. He was rude with people, aggressive in his stance and misbehaved with his colleagues in meetings.

People watched him for few months. One day some managers came together and complained to the King. The King too had noticed the young man's attitude shift. He called the young man for a discussion and asked, 'Do you feel what I've heard is correct? I'm asking you directly since I am responsible for placing you in the leadership team.'

The young man said, 'Your highness, only passionate people who care for the company argue, and I think I have every right to say what I mean.'

The King smiled and said very softly, 'Young man, you are right. You have every right to put forward your views. I always encourage that.'

'Then what are we discussing so late in the evening?' asked the young man, quite arrogantly.

'Nothing, I'm just observing how a little change in behaviour can ruin a career.'

The young man got a jolt. The King said, 'You have built your career through hard work and ability. Please do not ruin it. I have watched you very closely, you have certainly changed. Just a suggestion—stop being aggressive. Be assertive, and everything will be fine.'

'It does not work, your highness. I have tried hard in the past to request politely but no one listens to me. That is why I take this tough stance.'

'I'm surprised to note that, and the reason for that may be something else, but you definitely need to be assertive. Be self-assured, be confident and people will listen to you. By being aggressive, you are losing your content. People get scared of you and they act in self-defence. As a result, no discussion gets concluded. People still tolerate you because of your track record, but that may not last for too long!'

The young man listened carefully, as the King said, 'Please take my advice and things will be fine. We need the "old you" back.' The young man understood the problem and corrected himself quickly. And he lived happily ever after.

This is easier said than done. Assertiveness is an art that we need to master. It is probably one of the most important traits the corporate world demands. Many of you know that you need to be assertive, but you often forget that rule.

Through the day, you are constantly communicating. You are communicating even when you are silent. You need to be conscious all the time. A great analysis or a great idea is wasted if others do not understand its value. They will only understand its value when you communicate with them correctly, when you take them along with you in your journey.

You can be aggressive or passive in your communication. Both modes of communication are common. Aggressive behaviour is never appreciated. It can be intimidating; it creates bad blood between parties and finally leads to conflict or a situation of disagreement, which can lead to a deadlock. Most corporates discourage such behaviour, as it spoils the atmosphere of the organization. On the other hand, a passive communicator may be termed as too soft to be able to put forward his point or defend an argument. Often, these people are not deemed effective and might be considered pushovers.

Assertiveness follows a middle path. It is about making a point without hurting others' feelings. It is considered the right form of interaction in a corporate, or even otherwise in life. It reflects confidence in a person, helps the team arrive at decisions and allows everybody to voice their opinions, leading to a consensus, since it works through mutual trust and respect.

It's very easy to slip into an aggressive or a passive mode. The trick is to remain assertive, all the time, and master the art as quickly as possible. And to be assertive, you need to master the art of listening. After many years, I realized that the first step to listen is to be silent. It means being present with the person mentally. After many years, someone taught me that 'listen' and 'silent' have the same letters in them. I wondered why I didn't realize this earlier, even though I love to play with words.

Respect others

Men are respectable only as they respect.—Ralph Waldo Emerson

Once upon a time, the King, who was the owner of a company, called a young man to his palace for dinner. The young man was elated and honoured by the invitation. He felt so proud that he decided to bring his mother along. The King agreed.

The young man was bright and passionate about his work. In the last few months, he had also contributed heavily to the company's success. But he had a problem. He was extremely unpopular. Most people around him did not like him. The reason for that, more often than not, was that the young man was rude to others. He had no empathy for anyone. His behaviour in meetings and public forums was unacceptable. People hated his presence, as he often ended up having fights or getting drawn into endless arguments.

He had been often counselled by his seniors but he argued, saying, 'So what if people do not like me? I work here neither for popularity nor for an individual. I work for the company. I will say and do whatever is right for the company.'

Members of the senior management hated him, and felt that keeping him in the company was a nuisance. They requested the King's permission to sack this young man. The King assured his Ministers that he would take care of the situation. The Ministers did not like the King's response; they thought he was not taking their complaints seriously.

On the day of the invitation, as the young man was getting ready for the dinner, he heard a knock at the door. He saw a man from the King's office. The man informed him that the King had sent his car to receive the young man and his mother. The young man was elated, and his mother felt proud of her son.

As he entered the palace, the young man saw the King waiting at the gate to receive them. The King escorted them to the living room where the young man found the King's family waiting for them. During the conversation, he learnt that the King had a humble background and had built his entire empire on his own. The young man and his mother wondered how the King had become one of the top fifty rich people the country. During the conversation, the mother asked the King, 'Your highness, tell us the secret behind your success.'

The King said, 'I am no different from any of you. But when I look back, I realize—if anything is different in me, it is my respect for others. I never cared about what level someone was in, or what their economic condition was. I always knew that everyone could contribute to my learning and success. Hence I listen to others carefully, embrace every opinion, evaluate them before deciding on the next steps. Even today, when I know I am the King, I treat everybody with equality and esteem.'

The mother smiled. The King said to the young man, 'You have enough potential, but please remember these words. You can be extremely passionate at work, you may be the most intelligent person on this earth but you cannot survive alone. You need to learn how to move along with others, respect them, get them on to your side. This can only happen when you decide to communicate with respect and inclusion. Words that leave your mouth cannot be retrieved. You need to master this art, young man. You need to be careful all the time.'

The King treated them to a lavish dinner and the young man got the lesson of his life. And he lived happily ever after.

Being humble and respectful towards others is easier said than done. These traits have to come from within and should be expressed in the right way for people to understand. At the end of the day, you deal with people. Without them, you are nothing. You are here to run a business, take the company forward. You need to express what you feel or what you know.

If you watch successful people from various fields carefully, you will find one common element in them—most of them are modest and self-aware. A lion need not roar to prove that it is a lion. They know how to put across their viewpoints, they are able to make others agree to their perspectives, yet they remain humble and respectful towards others. They know when to give up and they agree with the others when they see that their points of view are more logical. To remain humble and respectful means having control over oneself all the time. This means keeping our emotions in check, being objective to the cause.

Corporate life is different from college life, where what you said did not affect your careers. Now, in this jungle, every word counts. Every move counts. People will act for or against you judging by the way you behave. Thus you need to be doubly sure of yourselves before you act. Respect also means showing responsibility towards others' needs and responding on time. It means taking criticism in your stride, as also taking the blame for your failure. People will appreciate someone who empathizes. To get respect, it is imperative to give respect. Being humble and respectful is a non-negotiable trait.

Maintain your integrity

Real integrity is doing the right thing, knowing that nobody's going to know whether you did it or not.—Oprah Winfrey

Once upon a time, there was a King who was the sales head of a company. He was on a recruitment spree, as the company was growing rapidly. His only job was to push his Ministers to get the right people into the company as soon as possible.

The company was divided into four regions: East, West, South, and North. The King noted a surprising trend—the region head for West was unable to recruit people, while others were filling up vacancies fast. When the King inquired with HR, he got different explanations, including how the competition was paying higher salaries in the West and how the talent market was so hot in the West that candidates were not interested in their company. But the King was not satisfied, since no one could provide him with a concrete answer. He couldn't find the real reason.

Some months passed by but the situation did not improve. The King decided to get involved himself. He asked the HR department to call the applicants directly to the head office, so that he could meet them before they met the region head. He also advised the HR department not to disclose the location of posting to the applicants; depending on their potential, the King would decide where to place them. He took this step as he guessed that he would not be able to attract the right candidates if he let it be known that they were being interviewed for jobs in the West.

One day, a young lady walked into the King's office. After an hour of interaction, the King offered her a job in the West. She immediately declined the job offer.

'But you are from Mumbai. Your parents live there, and I'm offering you a job in your hometown. You should be happy. Why are you declining the offer?' asked the King.

'Your highness, your logic is right, but I don't work for people who have had integrity issues.'

'What do you mean?' asked the surprised King.

'I said what I should not have said, I won't say anything further,' said the young lady.

But when King offered her a job in the East, she readily accepted.

Shocked to see her decision, the King inquired further, but discreetly. Through his personal contacts, he went into the past record of the West regional head, and found that he had been sacked many years ago by a previous employer on grounds of doubtful integrity. The King then went back to HR to check the region head's personal file. He discovered that he was recruited at the suggestion of the earlier King—without a reference check!

The King called the region head for a discussion and the latter confessed. 'But, your highness, that incident happened many years ago. I have changed since then,' he pleaded.

'That doesn't matter,' replied the King. 'First of all, you have concealed the fact and that is good enough reason for us not to continue with your employment. Second, as a policy, we do not employ people who have had integrity issues. Third, your act will haunt you throughout your life. So good luck, young man,' said the King, as the region head handed over his resignation. And he never lived happily after.

Once you are marked as a person of questionable integrity, your reputation will haunt you forever. Integrity is all about the intention to do what is right, honest, sincere. It talks about an integral part of one's character, value system, mindset.

In the corporate world, integrity is an indispensable trait. It does not matter whether a person succeeds or fails in his career; once he or she compromises on his values even for a day, and once his or her integrity is questioned, he or she ceases to exist in the corporate world.

Success is important but not at the cost of integrity. We must do everything to pursue our dream, try all means to achieve our goal, but not unethically. Money, power and position matter, but they must be obtained in the right way. There is no shortcut to success and it should never be achieved at the cost of our values.

Many people think that integrity is all about not stealing company money. Wrong! It can be as simple as not keeping a commitment. It is about doing things the right way. It is about adherence to moral and ethical practices. It is all about 'you' as a person and the way you think and act.

The region head in this story didn't imagine that his past deeds would haunt him forever. He did everything to correct himself and move ahead in life. Yet the King did not pardon him, as the corporate world always looks for undaunted and un-sacrificed integrity. He suffered for something he did years ago. You need to adhere to your value system from the day you arrive in this corporate jungle.

Stay positive

When you realize how perfect everything is, you will throw back your head and laugh at the sky.—The Buddha

Once upon a time, the King, who had just been appointed the operations head of a multi-billion-dollar company, was being interviewed by a young journalist. The interview progressed well; it was being telecast live on the nation's most popular channel. The young journalist posed some very tough questions but the King tackled them with ease. Almost at the end of the half-hour slot, the young man asked, 'Your highness, may I ask you a personal question?'

The King smiled and nodded.

To everyone's surprise, the young man asked, 'Your highness, you are not qualified enough to get this job. You do not have the coveted degrees that it demands. What made you reach here?'

The King replied, 'There are many things behind this success. It is difficult to single them out.'

'But I request you to come up with that "one thing".'

'I've stayed positive throughout my life.'

'We have little time, but do explain . . .'

'It is the way you look at something that determines your attitude. A glass can be half full or half empty, depending on the way you think.'

'I agree, but how do you keep yourself so positive despite all the issues you might face in running such large corporations?'

'Simple. It is because I *want* to stay positive. I think

positive, talk positive, read positive, watch positive! In simple words, I keep myself surrounded by all the positive elements, hence I act positive. It is important for me, people around me will get affected. Both negative and positive attitudes are contagious. Negativity is like a disease. I do not want it to spread. I am responsible for so many lives—at home, in my office. I cannot afford to spoil them. The fun is in keeping this positive attitude throughout life. Things don't always go the way we want them to and that can push us to think negatively. A winner stays positive even in such circumstances.'

The King smiled and said, 'Young man, stay positive and you will live well and succeed too.'

At the end of the show, the young man smiled and said, 'Thank you, your highness! I think this interview is enough for me to make myself live happily ever after.'

I strongly believe in the fact that one's attitude gives one the altitude one would like to attain. Positivity is the trait that helps you move ahead, looking at the brighter side of life. It gives you energy, courage, optimism. It gives you an edge over the others. It is the difference between starting work thinking: 'It will be done,' as opposed to 'It may not be done.' When you start a journey with the mindset that it will be completed, the journey will be so much fun.

A positive state of mind is always encouraged. It is a state that allows you to think constructively and not miss out on possible options and solutions. It gives you a never-say-die attitude, makes you stronger from within, allows you to take risks and enables us to take certain decisions that we would never take in a negative frame of mind. It helps us discover opportunities.

Any sincere effort will yield success, but when you make the effort with a positive attitude, it makes the journey through corporate life so much more meaningful and fulfilling. It allows you to lead teams of people better, gives you the right attitude to deal with everybody in and around your life, be it in the corporate world or otherwise.

Positivity spreads naturally. A person with positive energy is always better liked than one with negativity. It helps you have faith in yourself, and have faith in people around you. It is easy to think negatively. But when you think positively, you do a lot of good for ourselves and for the world around you by demonstrating the can-do attitude.

It is important to maintain this positive attitude throughout life. Things may not always go the way we want them to but a winner stays positive constantly.

If there are two individuals with equal competence, the person with more positivity is bound to move ahead of the other. Stay positive from the very first day in your career.

Look beyond the analysis

You must trust the small voice inside you which tells you exactly what to say, what to decide.—Ingrid Bergman

Once upon a time, there was a young man who joined his father's manufacturing business. This young man was a qualified engineer and always wanted to join a large corporate. However, he had to take the decision to join the family business due to his father's ill-health. There was no one else to take on the mantle.

The company was into manufacturing of high-precision components and supplied to a major automotive manufacturer. During the time that the young man joined, the company was going through a major crisis; the rejection level of a component, which contributed almost 50 per cent of the sales, was going up every month. The situation worsened when one of the lots got completely rejected by the buyer. The reason for rejection was 'oversized, not fitting properly'.

The problem was explained to this young man. Being an engineer, he decided to solve the problem himself. He went down to the shop floor, inspected components and tools against the drawings and revalidated the processes, but was unable to find any error. He repeated the exercise a few times, but the result was no different. Convinced that the rejection of components was a wrong move by the buyer, he decided to meet them.

Despite a long meeting with the managers of the automotive manufacturer, the young man was unable to convince them with his logic. The managers had enough evidence to prove him wrong. Frustrated, he visited the shop floor again and met the operators, only to realize that the components indeed had some dimension issues. However, no one could pinpoint the problem. In fact, the problem differed from component to component.

The young man was hell-bent on solving the problem

this time. He worked relentlessly for a few days, but did not make much progress. The next lot too was rejected. The young man challenged the buyer and sent across a legal notice for harassment. The relationship worsened so much that the buyer stopped all payments and suspended all orders.

The young man met his father—the King—for advice. The King heard him out, smiled and said, 'Don't worry, my son. Meet Ramu Kaka. He will solve the issue for you.'

'But who is Ramu Kaka?' asked the arrogant young man.

'He is my guru. He made me what I am today. He is one of the oldest operators in the factory.'

The young man left the palace and he decided not to meet Ramu Kaka. He was not convinced that a mere operator could resolve a problem that an engineer could not. He was confident that his engineering degree would help him resolve the issue. He asked some of his friends for help. All of them struggled for a week, but were unable to make any headway. With no money flowing in, the company faced a cash crunch. The situation was grim.

With no option in hand, the young man thought of the last probable ray of hope. He called Ramu Kaka to his office and explained the issue. He gave Ramu Kaka two days to come up with the solution. Ramu Kaka did not utter a word and left.

The next day, as the young man entered his office, he found Ramu Kaka waiting for him. To his surprise, he realized that Ramu Kaka had found a solution that he and his brilliant friends could not. Production changes were made, based on Ramu Kaka's advice, and the next batch was dispatched. The young man rushed to the buyer and apologized for his behaviour. Supplies resumed and no lot ever got rejected again.

When the young man asked Ramu Kaka how he found the solution, he answered, 'Young man, I can see beyond those drawings and numbers.'

The company survived and the young man learnt a big lesson. He lived happily ever after.

Often, when encountered with a problem, you stop thinking and don't look beyond a certain analysis. You get bogged down by that mundane analysis and stop thinking creatively. You get stuck in the same loop of data and fail to find an answer for yourselves.

When data is presented to us, we all look at it from different perspectives. That is natural, since each one of us is a different individual with differing experiences, backgrounds, education and knowledge. What is interesting is that, in the same situation and from the same data, some people can find a solution even as others stare at the numbers helplessly. This happens when you can look beyond numbers, when you can really understand the analyses. There is a certain bent of mind that makes one look at new avenues to solve problems. There is no magic formula to this trait—it is about the acumen and insight that you either possess naturally or develop through experience. This attribute differentiates you from others.

This is what happened to the young man. He had all the logic and analyses to believe that he was producing the right component, but he failed to look beyond the numbers. Ramu Kaka did that for him and found the solution that saved the business. Some call it out-of-the-box thinking, some may call it a radical approach, some may call it sheer intuition, but the person who possesses this trait can be a real gift to the business. And this is one quality that is not always inborn. Over time, you all can become 'Ramu Kaka' by developing a sense for that which lies 'beyond'.

Use your common sense

I can never fear that things will go far wrong where common sense has fair play.—Thomas Jefferson

Once upon a time, there was a young lady who was the recruitment manager for an airline. One day, she was travelling to recruit an investor relationship manager who would be responsible for, among other things, mergers and acquisitions. During the interview, she got a phone call from the HR head about a girl being recommended by the King, the director of the company. The HR head told her to recruit this girl, even if she did not meet all the recruitment standards.

At that time, the company was looking for funds and was talking to investors. This position was the key contact for all such discussions. In fact, some proposals were at an advanced stage of negotiation and only a few people in the company were aware of thos developments. This young lady, being part of the recruitment team, knew of the companies the airline was talking to.

The young lady interviewed the recommended candidate and found her extremely suitable, yet she rejected her. In a few days, back at the head office, she met the HR head. The HR head was furious, as by then, the news had reached the King. The King was offended that his instruction had not been followed. The young lady did not react but requested an audience with the King. She said to the HR head, 'Please have patience. I will explain my stance to both of you in the meeting. I am sure you will appreciate my decision.'

After a few hours, when she met the King, he expressed his frustration. After hearing him out patiently, the young lady said, 'Sir, I care for the company as well as for you, hence I took my decision. Before I went for the recruitment process, you had explained to me the importance of this position. You also told me that if news of the probable merger leaked out, you and the airline would be in serious trouble.'

'Yes, I did tell you that, but how does it link up with the lady I recommended?'

'It has a connection, your highness, which is why I took such a bold decision at the risk of my career. I would certainly say that, for this position, technically she was the best candidate I met. However, during the interview process, she revealed that her boyfriend had joined one of the companies that we are talking to for divestment. She also told me that they live together and plan to get married next month. I knew she would maintain a high degree of confidentiality, but I did not want to take a chance.

If she, in a weak moment, revealed something about the deal, we could be in a soup. I thought it better to be safe than sorry, hence the decision. If you still think that I was wrong and wrongfully violated your advice, I will accept any punishment.'

The King looked at her and said, 'I am glad you took that decision. It was just common sense, wasn't it?' The HR head and the King were happy and the young lady lived happily ever after.

As is often said, it is true that common sense is the most uncommon sense to find. Most of us either do not believe in it or do not want to use it. To me, common sense is a knowledge that we all acquire over time, gained from this world through education and experience. Often, it may not be logical, but it works.

Often, it happens to be that despite all logical analyses and arguments, we still do not agree with certain decisions and may opt for a different route. We disagree, as something within us does not allow us to agree with the facts and figures. At times, we take radical decisions and steps based on 'something' that we fail to define. This is when we believe in and rely on our common sense. It's all about simple thinking, which is logical.

Of course, I do not want to suggest that we all should live by our gut instinct and ignore all logic. Common sense is not a substitute for data or logic. It is a sense that can help us revalidate decisions. It acts as a gatekeeper to help us act in the right way.

In the case of the young lady too, all data suggested that she should have recruited the recommended candidate, but her common sense stopped her. And she turned out to be right, as that step would have put the company at too much risk. Both the King and the HR head appreciated her decision. The more we understand the importance of common sense, the better our journey through the corporate jungle will be.

Learn to negotiate

Let us never negotiate out of fear. But let us never fear to negotiate.—John F. Kennedy

Once upon a time, there was a King who ran a contract packing operation for a multinational. His job was to produce on behalf of the company, based on agreed specifications. In return, he earned a commission.

The King was a senior professional, highly respected in the industry. People knew him as a self-made man; his was the typical rags-to-riches story we see in films. After many years, the King retired and handed over operations to the next generation.

It was October, the time when the company negotiated the next year's rates with the contract packers. There was a young man in that multinational in charge of finalizing the contract packing agreements. When people from the King's company were called to the head office to finalize their contract, the young man was surprised to find the King present with his two sons. He welcomed the King and initiated discussions. Both the parties went into detailed discussions, analysing each cost item threadbare. The meeting lasted for almost eight hours and, finally, the young man proposed a price that he thought the King and his team would agree to.

While the body language of his sons showed that they were satisfied with the offered rate, the old man rejected it. The young man said, 'But, your highness, the difference is only about 1 per cent, which means 25 paise per unit. You are such a big businessman—how can such a tiny amount make a difference to you?'

The King replied, 'Young man, my children don't understand the value of this small amount and neither do you.' He paused for a moment and said, 'When I started my career, I had no money; I used to work as a daily wage-earner. Today, I have few hundred crores. The difference between me and the others was this little amount. All those 25 paise have made me what I am today.'

The young man did not understand much of what the King said. For him, it was more important to close the deal that day since his boss asked him to do so. He said, 'Sir, I need to close the deal today, I really don't think that 25 paise would make any difference to a large company like ours.'

The King smiled and signed the deal. Before he left the young man's office, he said, 'Young man, a piece of advice for you. What you did today is not good for your company. Your attitude will ruin your company some day. I appreciate your sense of urgency, but not your ignorance of the value of money. If you want to move ahead in the corporate world, you need to negotiate better.'

The young man kept that advice in mind, which helped him in all his future negotiations. He lived happily ever after.

Great negotiators don't possess the quality from birth, but master the art over time. We are negotiating in every moment in life, be it in office or elsewhere. We are negotiating with our colleagues, friends, families, strangers and, if not with anyone else, ourselves. Negotiation is not only about money, it is about everything around you. That's what life is all about. Negotiation is not a luxury but a necessity for anyone to survive in this world. People who understand the art of negotiation are the people who add value to the business.

If we believe that only finance professionals handle finance and only procurement and supply chain staff need to negotiate, we are wrong. Everybody in the corporate world negotiates all the time. Let us look at a few examples. Do you think that a frontline salesman does not negotiate? We may think that his job is to meet dealers, get orders, communicate prices and supply stocks. Let us look at his job more closely. Every moment, within the company or outside the company, he is negotiating. Within the company, he is negotiating for stocks, discounts, pricing. Outside the company, he is negotiating for orders, shelf space and so on. Or let us take the example of a production manager. He negotiates with his team all the time for higher productivity and better quality, and also with his higher-ups for extra budgets and plant overhauls.

The King understood the value for money. Even a few paise were important for him. He was negotiating for that extra profit. He was personally present in the meeting, as he knew that his sons had not yet understood the value of these few extra paise.

The art of negotiation applies across functions, jobs, designations. In life, everybody is negotiating all the time, though for varying purposes since the resources are limited and the opportunities are unlimited. How can you be a great manager if you do not master this art?

Stay updated

I don't think much of a man who is not wiser today than he was yesterday.—Abraham Lincoln

Once upon a time, there were two young women who joined a large corporation as management trainees. One of them came from a small town and had studied in a vernacular school. The other hailed from a large metro and had been educated in a premier boarding school. She had excellent communication skills, knew how to deal with people, and was very high on confidence. For the small-town girl, this was the first exposure to city life. She was shy and quiet and often avoided the public glare. She knew that she needed to develop her skills to suit the corporate atmosphere.

The small-town girl was awestruck by the city girl when they met. She liked everything about her from their very first interaction. She was in awe of her smartness, her communication skills and her ability to negotiate the corporate world. As they say, opposites attract. Soon they became good friends and decided to share an accommodation.

The small-town girl always wondered what gave the city girl such confidence and guessed that it was probably growing up in a big city or living in a hostel independently that shaped her personality. For her, it was an opportunity to observe the best from a close distance and she was ready to learn. The small-town girl knew her own weak areas and found a mentor in the city girl.

The city girl, in a way, had a know-it-all attitude. She knew her strengths and always liked to be appreciated. Being friends with the small-town girl suited her, as she found a person to whom she could constantly show off; the small-town girl was always eager to listen to her.

The small-town girl had several good qualities. She had an open mind and was ready to take on any challenge. She wanted to learn more than her job, so she moved about, met people from other departments and quickly learnt a lot about the business.

She listened to others and learnt from everyone around her. She wanted to share some of her learning with the city girl, but all her efforts landed on a deaf ear. The city girl considered herself one up against the rest—learning from others was not something she would even consider.

Time passed by and, one day, the city girl was called by the King, her boss. He said, 'I expected much more from you. But I am disappointed.'

The city girl never anticipated a blow like that. She thought she was smart enough to impress anyone. When she inquired further, her boss shared: 'Shed your know-it-all attitude. It is so obvious. It does not work in a corporate. You need to change, my little girl. It looks like you have stopped working on yourself.'

She asked, 'But, your highness, what went wrong?'

'Nothing, except for the fact that you've stopped learning! You've stopped developing yourself. Your overconfidence is taking you backwards. Look at your friend. I'm amazed at the way she has developed herself. She has completely transformed herself in the last year. She beams with confidence now. Who can tell now that she once had so many shortcomings?'

'But sir, she had those problems, so she had to learn. I was perfect!'

The King laughed and said, 'She worked on herself in the areas she felt challenged. She put in that extra effort to overcome her shortcomings. Not only that, she moved around to gather knowledge beyond her area. She is preparing herself for the next level. That is why I'm talking so highly of her. You cannot evolve unless you have the urge within you to find your own shortcomings. Else you will miss the opportunity to hone your talents. You have to be different and ahead of others in all aspects—that is how you should differentiate yourself. Use every opportunity.'

The city girl listened carefully. The King added, 'You must thank your parents for sending you to one of the best schools. Very few people are privileged to get such an opportunity. But that does not mean that you have all the knowledge in this world. Keep learning, keep growing. That is the only way to success.' The city girl agreed to change, and lived happily ever after.

'The more, the merrier' should be your mantra when it comes to learning. As we discussed earlier, you may have to 'undo' a lot and learn new things. We must keep updating ourselves, be it for subject knowledge or for soft skills. Rediscover yourself as a 'corporate absorber' or a 'habitual learner'. The more you absorb in these few years, the better your chance to succeed.

Move around, meet people, watch them. Ask them the smartest as well as the silliest questions you want to ask. Trust me, no one will mind that, at this stage of your career. This is your opportunity to ask as much as you want, to learn as much as you desire. You are here to become the future CEOs. How will you be the one if you do not acquire the desired knowledge?

You may be new to the corporate world . . . So what? Try and learn as much as you want. What's wrong in expressing your intention to work on a strategy encompassing the next three years? What stops you from learning about how the resources are allocated? Why not spend time to understand how the procurement department negotiates with vendors? Why not work on annual budgeting? Won't it be interesting to learn from your friends about how a new outlet is opened? Or how a presentation for the board of directors is prepared? Why not watch a senior leader making a presentation? The list can go on . . . You may learn formally or informally from interactions. It does not matter how you acquire knowledge—what matters is your urge to learn, to expand your skill set.

Always remember that your hunger for knowledge and your willingness to update yourself will differentiate you from your colleagues. In any organization, overall knowledge is valued and appreciated more than subject knowledge; it will put your career on the fast-track mode. It will be the biggest differentiator.

The small-town girl knew her weaknesses and worked on them systematically to overcome her shortcomings. On the other hand, the city girl's progress suffered due to her overconfidence and her unwillingness to update her skills. Never ever allow this hunger to die—it is your visa for a fast-track career. The sooner you realize this, the better it is for your career.

Enjoy every day

And in the end, it's not the years in your life that count. It's the life in your years.—Abraham Lincoln

Once upon a time, there was a young lady who joined a company's quality department. The factory she joined was in a hot and humid city. Her job demanded that she be out in the sun at the factory warehouse to check the quality of outgoing products. It was a difficult job, especially in the simmering summer.

She was a diligent worker, always focused and busy. Her colleagues admired her dedication. While every other employee in the quality department had a tired face at the end of the day, this young lady was always fresh and happy. She never complained of her workload or the tough working conditions. In fact, with every passing hour of the day, she looked more energetic. No one could understand the reason and soon the lady became a topic of discussion in the factory.

The news reached the King, the factory head.

The King wanted to meet the young lady to understand her better. One day, he visited her office late in the afternoon, without any advance intimation. The King watched the young lady from a distance and could not believe his eyes. Even in the scorching sun, she was full of energy, inspecting every product diligently.

The King went back quietly, but invited her for lunch the next day. What the young lady told him was amazing. She said, 'Your highness, I'm here to work and make a career for myself. Hence it is important for me to love my job. I need to utilize my time the best I can. As I work, with every passing hour, I feel better as I feel closer to my goal.'

The King could not understand the philosophy behind the young girl's words and asked again, 'Please explain to me further, young lady. I am eager!'

The young lady replied, 'Your highness, I feel confident as I learn new things and deliver new results. This encourages me to do better the next day. As I finish my day with new learning and experience, I look forward to charge back the next day, to deliver more. This is the secret of my behaviour and energy.'

The King was amazed and asked, 'But don't you feel tired?'

'No, your highness. I enjoy my work every moment. I know I can easily shift to a cushy job but then I will never get the hands-on experience of the shop floor. Here, every day, I face new issues and when I solve them, I feel elated. It is a golden opportunity. Why should I lose this pleasure even for a single moment?'

The King patted the young girl on her back and they lived happily ever after.

Each day is different. Some days help us charge ahead, some pull us down. On some, we make mistakes, on some we don't. In some we learn, in some we teach . . . Life goes on inexorably but enjoying every day is in our control. We should not miss that opportunity.

The demand on us is to deliver results each day and we need to do that, while sustaining our positivity. Emotions affect us in a big way; ups and downs at work or at home affect our minds. The trick is to look ahead, enjoy the moment and deliver our best every day. This will give us the strength to do more without realizing how difficult it was.

At the end of our careers, when we look back, we will realize how each and every day had shaped our lives. If we have reached our goals by enjoying each day, our journeys must have been pleasant. It is an art to look forward to the next day with equal ambition and zeal to perform. Each day will add to our experience and we will be rich in learning at the end of it.

The first few years in the corporate world are important for us to build our future, and we need to stay focused. When we have the chance to move closer to our goals by performing every day, why compromise that enjoyment?

***

Today's session was a little shorter than the last one. Mr Chatterjee wanted it that way. He took a deep breath and said, 'In a corporate, we all come from different backgrounds, education levels and competence. It does not matter how good or how bad you were in college. It is just a few years of formal education versus many years of career-building. It does not matter how we start but we should keep our eye firmly on where we want to reach. It is important to see our target clearly every day as we reach our workplace. Let us not lose sight of our goals. Each day, as we deliver results, we will drive towards our destiny, a destiny we have defined for ourselves. Let us take each day as a project and let us perform as if there is no tomorrow.'

He paused and added, 'That's all for today. I want you to think about what we discussed in the last three weeks before we meet for our last session. That will be another important day, since we will finally learn how to emerge as winners from the jungle. Over the next few days, please reflect on what we have spoken till now. Before we end today, as usual, let us summarize our learning.'

A participant took the lead and said, 'Vivek, to start with, we understood the importance of asking the right questions.'

Mr Chatterjee said, 'Well, we also learnt the importance of asking the wrong question. We must keep learning till we drop dead!'

We all laughed as another participant said, 'We learnt how to communicate.'

'Not really,' said Mr Chatterjee. 'We never learnt how to communicate. What we understood was the importance of right communication. Learning how to communicate is probably the biggest lesson we all need to extract as we travel through the jungle.'

The participant nodded.

I said, 'Sir, we also spoke about staying positive, always. We learnt how positivity spreads.'

'We also spoke about integrity. I think this is one trait which is imperative to survive in the jungle each and every day,' said another.

'Absolutely! Let us be true to ourselves all the time, doing the right things in the right way,' said Mr Chatterjee.

'We also spoke about the importance of number sense, common sense and how important it is to master the art of negotiation. Today I realize why my parents were so persistent in pushing me for my mathematics classes.'

Mr Chatterjee smiled and said, 'You must appreciate that none of these traits can work in isolation. We need to master all of them. And we need to enjoy every day as we master these traits. They will do wonders for us. These are the qualities we will always need, as we navigate our way to the top.'

Mr Chatterjee looked at me and said, 'I won't ask you right now whether you are convinced.'

I did not answer. But I knew he was right. I was convinced by now that the first few years can make or break a career. I felt bad that these sessions were coming to an end. But I did what I had just learnt—I thought positive and said to myself that all good things come to an end but the learning stays with us for life.

I took my empty glass, raised a toast and said, 'Cheers to my first few years!'

SECTION 4

EMERGING AS A WINNER
FROM THE JUNGLE

The next Saturday, as we met in the morning, Mr Chatterjee said, 'Today, we will end our sessions, but, before we end, it is important to understand why some people emerge as winners, while some don't, despite knowing all they need to succeed. But, as I promised earlier, we will go on till I am able to convince you all.'

One of us said, 'We won't mind, sir! We are enjoying every moment we spend together.'

'Thank you. I am thankful to all of you as you have shown enough maturity and presence in the last few sessions.' He paused and said, 'As I said, I will try to end these sessions today. It will be a long session and we will not break in between. I have requested for a working lunch. I hope that suits you.'

We all agreed, as we wanted to grab as much knowledge as we could. 'Finally, we will summarize the lessons of the day and then ask ourselves one big question. I will let you know the big question at the end,' said Mr Chatterjee.

As we wondered what that would be, Mr Chatterjee started with his stories.

Network intelligently

More business decisions occur over lunch and dinner than at any other time, yet no MBA courses are given on the subject.
—Peter Drucker

Once upon a time, there was a King, the CEO of a company. He was a man of few words. Formal and a bit introverted, he did not share his thoughts with many people. He wanted to keep the company's strategies safe.

One day, he was surprised to hear that a decision regarding a price reduction—which was taken just the day before—had reached the competition even before he had the opportunity to roll that out to the market. The King felt frustrated, he knew it was a grand move to take the competition by surprise.

The decision was taken in a meeting with about seven people being present. Had he made a mistake by discussing an important strategy with such a large number of people, he wondered. But then, they were his senior employees, and he needed to trust them!

The King was upset and decided to go to the bottom of the issue. He wanted to ensure that a lesson was taught to the culprit who had leaked the news, so that the same is not repeated ever again. He called a special meeting of his direct subordinates, to discuss the matter. The meeting lasted a few hours, but not much could be achieved, since every leader was clueless. The King finally asked the HR head to investigate.

The HR head decided to look at the telephone calling

patterns of all the people present at the earlier meeting. He zeroed down on three managers who called the competitor's office regularly. He met those three managers for interrogations. All of them came back with the excuse that they had old friends in the competitor's office, and they had every right to talk to their friends. The HR head could not find fault with their logic.

When this result was presented to the King, he was not too happy, and asked, 'Who among these three is the most networked guy?'

'What do you mean by that, your highness?' asked the HR head.

'Who moves around, meets people, parties every other night, attend meetings in different forums?'

The HR head thought for a while and named one among them. The King suspected that this young man can be the culprit. When that young man was interrogated further, he succumbed to the investigation committee.

When asked why, he said, 'Your highness, I had no intention to harm the organization. Yesterday night, I called few ex-colleagues home. One of them now works for our competitor. We were discussing several issues—one of the topics was the recent market slowdown. Most of my friends were of the opinion that one should never drop the price of a product in difficult situations, since it would have a direct effect on the profitability. I argued back and during that time I referred to our decision to take down the price in the next few days. I'm sorry that I could not understand the implication of my deed. Today I know how big a fool I am and how dangerous the disease of networking can be, if not done in the right manner.'

The young man resigned voluntarily. For many years, he did not live happily.

It is often said that your progress depends not on how much you know, but who are the people you know. Knowing people helps, and knowing the right people helps more. Hence there is no doubt that one needs to network both within the company and outside.

Networking has both pros and cons. It can take a toll on you, as it requires you to invest enough time and energy, and we all know that both these resources are precious as well as limited. Hence we need to be clear about whom we want to network with and why. Focus on the people who matter, people who can add value to your personal and professional life.

Every company has its own written or unwritten rules. For example, in some organization talking to competition employees is a clear no-no, while some organizations allow you but guide you about how to act and be with certain boundaries in such circumstances. Similar rules will also exist for internal networking. You need to develop a clear understanding of the dos and the don'ts. You certainly need to know what is confidential and cannot be disclosed, what not to say before your friends in the office, etc. The list can be long, but for effective networking, you must take an effort to know them.

As I said, there is nothing wrong to know or be known to people. But be careful in your interactions, lest you are termed as a networker who wastes time or cannot be trusted. Have a clear agenda and goal for networking activity and focus on the desired outcome. There is a thin line between networking and gossiping. Just be mindful of that line. The sooner you learn this, the better are your chances to emerge as a winner from this jungle.

Take risks

Impossible is a word to be found only in the dictionary of fools.—Napoleon Bonaparte

Once upon a time, there was a young man who did not like his job. He felt that he had landed in the wrong career. He had dreamt of becoming an ad filmmaker but, thanks to his parents' wishes, he ended up in an engineering college, followed it up with an MBA, followed by a corporate HR job as a compensation and benefit manager. He never thanked his parents for his engineering or management degrees. He hated his job and always wondered why he had listened to his parents. He felt he would have been happier by earning half his salary as a struggling filmmaker—at least he would have done what he always cherished. He often thought of quitting, but his father would not let him. He couldn't counter his father's arguments and logic—that chances of success in the film world were absolutely limited. The young man finally gave in, blaming his destiny.

In the office, the young man was popular, thanks to his role in compensation and benefits. Everybody knew of his interest in filmmaking, as he always spoke about his passion. Some encouraged him, but most of them laughed it off.

An opportunity came around for him when the company decided to shoot its new advertising campaign. That year, the company decided to move away from idea of a celebrity brand ambassador and feature its own employees in its advertisement. The concept was unique and everyone was excited. The marketing department received several applications from employees who aspired to become the brand ambassadors.

Sensing his opportunity, the young man approached the King, the head of marketing, and said, 'Sir, I have a request.'

'Yes, young man, tell me what I can do for you?'

'I know you are shooting our new advertisement.'

'Yes, do you want to become a brand ambassador?' asked the King.

'No, your highness. I want to shoot the film for you.'

The King laughed and said, 'You must be kidding, young man.'

'I mean it, your highness,' replied the young man firmly.

'That's great,' the King said, sarcastically. 'I never knew about this side of you, young man. So which was the last film you shot?'

'I did a few documentary films in college. I haven't shot an ad film yet,' replied the young man confidently.

'We are going to air the advertisement on national television. How can I allow you to shoot it?'

'I am confident, your highness. Please give me a chance. You won't be disappointed.'

The King thought for a moment and asked, 'What if you fail?'

'I will resign and return the cost to the company. In fact, you can take my resignation letter now.'

The King looked at the young man and said, 'I'm confused. No one has ever approached me with such a proposal. You are amazing!'

'Allow me, please. I won't let you down,' replied the young man.

The King thought for a while and said, 'I know I'm risking my job, but let's give it a try. My gut tells me that you will do well. In fact, if you are successful, I will ensure that people know about you. This will be our biggest talking point in the media. We will show the world how we recognize internal talent. But, if you fail, you will have to pay for it.'

His heart racing with joy, the young man said convincingly, 'I will not fail. When can we start?'

'Monday next.'

The young man left the King's office. The rest is history. The young man did a wonderful job and got lauded by one and all. After some years, he left his regular HR role to pursue his dream. Today he is one of the country's most renowned ad filmmakers. He also advises companies on HR policies . . . And he has lived happily ever after.

When was the last time you took a risk that impacted your education? It was probably the time when you decided on the subject stream to pursue—science, commerce, arts

... The time has come to reassess your risk-taking ability. We all know that success is relative and it is up to us to define success and our goals. These will be different for each individual. As we discussed earlier, once we define our goal, we have two choices. The first is the simple route, which leads to a simple career progression and may lead us to our goals some day.

The other route is to beat the normal curve. If we decide to choose the second option, we need to take risks. What I mean is that we need to take smart risks. If you are scared to take that smart risk, you may never gain big. Thus, it is important that we look at the positive side of risk-taking. Most organizations appreciate people who take the second route. I'm not suggesting that you should become a gambler, because slot machines may never yield jackpots. I'm talking about taking calculated risks. Weigh your options, do your homework, analyse the pros and cons of a situation before jumping into something.

At the same time, remember to prepare yourself for failure. After all, if you try, you may fail too. If you don't try, you won't have the chance to fail or succeed. If your risk backfires, some people will criticize you. So what? Take criticism in your stride; it will prepare you to take the next risk. It's your life, and you have every right to fail. It's your decision, so be proud of it. In this way, at least you will not repent at the end of your career.

That is what the young man did. He knew his passion. His ambition was to become an ad filmmaker. He believed in his capability and took the plunge to pursue his dream. It helped him to express his creative streak. His determination and zeal to do something he always wanted to do urged him on to succeed. The young man was fairly sure of himself; even if he had failed, the process would have satisfied his creative inner self.

The King too saw his passion and confidence and allowed him to experiment. It was an intelligent and calculated risk—even if the young man failed, the King had nothing to lose. He could have re-commissioned the film over the next few days. If the young man did a good job, however, it would become the talk of the industry. It was a win–win situation for both.

Go beyond the assigned job

Believe strongly in yourself and go beyond limitations.
—Arnold Schwarzenegger

Once upon a time, The King, the head of the commercial department of a large corporation, was in deep trouble. He had joined the organization a month ago and it was time to deliver the next year's profit plan. The King was not yet familiar with the business and depended heavily on his Minister, the second in command. The Minister, in turn, depended on a person known to be an expert at that task. The Minister was not a hands-on manager and had no clue how the job was to be done. All the assurances that he gave to the King were based on what the expert told him. The King was assured that the job would be completed before the deadline.

A day before the submission date, late at night, the King got a call from his Minister that the expert had a family problem and had to rush to his hometown. The Minister broke down and confessed that he had no clue about the progress of the job and that he could do little to salvage it without the expert around.

The King realized that he was in big trouble. His reputation would be at stake if the deadlines were not met. In despair, he asked the Minister and other members of his team to meet him immediately. After a short discussion, the King realized that the Minister could not be of any help to him. The King was exceedingly restless.

In a little while, a young man walked into his office and said, 'Your highness, I just heard about the situation. I have some idea of the job because my cubicle is just next to the expert. I overhear his conversation at times. If you allow me, can I try?'

The King looked at him and asked, 'I have no time left, young man. But, in this situation, I have no option but to agree with you.'

The young man replied confidently, 'Trust me, your highness, I will try my best. I will work overnight and report to you before you reach the office tomorrow. Even if I fail, you will not lose any time. The good news is that I have never failed in the past.'

The King smiled and was a bit relaxed. The young man worked terribly hard that night and completed the job. He saved the King tremendous embarrassment. The King remembered that forever, and they lived happily ever after.

Gone are the days when the moment you take up a job, you are handed a sheet of paper with your job description. Life has moved beyond the job description. We still get our one-page job description, but along with it comes another virtual bank paper, which stares at you every moment and asks you: 'What more?' It's a question that the employer asks us all the time; if not, we should ask ourselves every moment.

The world is changing, so is the corporate world. The competition among people to reach the top is heating up every day. We are here to reach the top. Let us go and grab the opportunity. Let us also take on some responsibility that may not be 'defined' for us. This not only secures a great career but also expands the horizon for us to take our skills beyond the explicit job description.

Life is all about demand and supply. The corporate world is no different. In our country of one billion people, it won't be difficult for an employer to look for another person with a similar background but with the willingness to fill up that virtual page that asks: 'What more?' Whether you get a salary raise or an early promotion by doing that extra bit is not important—what matters is the learning you take away from there and the reputation you build for yourself for the future. Look at this young man who went ahead to extend a helping hand to his King who was in dire straits. He stuck his neck out unconditionally, ignoring the fear of failure. He is bound to get rewarded, if not today then tomorrow. Start to stretch yourself beyond your stated job description the moment you arrive in this jungle.

Manage perceptions

Three things cannot be long hidden: the sun, the moon and the truth.—The Buddha

Once upon a time, there was a Minister, the marketing head of a large corporation. He was new in the system and had joined the company when they needed new thinking to turn it around. The company was going through a rough patch and the King, the CEO, hired this Minister specifically to help him turn around the company.

As he took over his new job, the Minister appointed two young men from his earlier association in his department. He hired them because they possessed certain skills that the company needed at that moment. The King was sceptical when the Minister wanted to get his 'own people' but agreed because he knew that the Minister was a man with unimpeachable integrity.

In a few months, the King was extremely pleased with these young men since they, along with the Minister, had contributed heavily to the progress of the company. They were awesome together and the entire company praised the overall contribution. However, other employees in the marketing department were not too happy that these two young men were given more importance than them, the 'older' employees. They got irritated when these two young men got promoted ahead of everyone else and were all set to become the seniormost associates in the department.

It took no time for people to form the perception that

the Minister was partial to his people, and favoured these young men. The news reached the Minister but he did not pay heed. He laughed, because he was sure of his own action. He had promoted them for their ability, not for their proximity to him!

The matter did not end there. The finance team lodged a complaint to the King, indicating the anarchy in the department and how the Minister favoured his two young men. They threatened to stop work unless the King took action against the Minister. The King asked the Minister for an explanation. The Minister explained his logic. The King accepted it and called the other folks in the marketing department to explain. He addressed them along with the Minister, assuring them that he would not tolerate anarchy in any department, leave alone marketing. The folks went back happy.

The King now turned and said to the Minister, 'I see the logic in your words but I never expected that you, being such a senior member of the management team, would fail to manage the image of your own team. I think you too have learnt something from this entire episode.' The Minister agreed, decided to manage his image better and lived happily ever after.

Your dreams and the reality do not always match, especially in the corporate world. There are days or weeks or even months when things can be really frustrating for you. You know that you are really doing well, but you may feel that you are not getting enough rewards. You may feel ignored and fret when you feel that no one is noticing your good work. A change in job profile that you are expecting may be offered to someone else. A foreign posting that you are ready for may be offered to your best friend in the office, and you may have no clue what went wrong with your candidature. All this may happen when you don't manage your image well.

It is true that in the end the truth will surface, and to make that happen you need to do a good job, every time. But you also need to manage perceptions all the time. It's like managing a brand. Even the best brands spend massively to maintain the brand position and image, reminding people every moment that they exist and that they are good.

In the corporate world, you are a brand of your own, and you need to manage it yourself. No advertising agency will do that for you. Thus it is absolutely necessary that people perceive you the way you want them to perceive you. Based on what you want people to think about you, you need to communicate the right things. If you aspire to evolve into the CEO from the CFO and if you do not talk business, you will always be termed as an accountant who manages his books well. Similarly, if you want to move from sales to marketing but if people perceive you as a hard-core sales guy pushing volumes all the time, your chances to move functions will be slim.

Perceptions are often created by the way you behave as a person but can also be formed through hearsay. Word of mouth plays a big role. For instance, if your conversations start with the word no, you may be termed as a negative person. If you tend to agree with whatever your boss says, you may be termed as a yes-man. It is about how people see you as a person.

Perceptions are perceptions. They may be true, they may be false. But, if not managed well, they may harm your career. Be alert all the time, talk to people, get their feedback and reflect on what people think about you. This will help you understand where you stand.

However, in this effort too, one needs to be careful. Over-managing your image, talking too much about your own achievements or pushing a goal too heavily may also create doubts in the minds of others and that may act against you. Master the art of managing your own brand.

In this story, the Minister should have acted when he heard the rumour or should have been thought twice before promoting those two young men. At the very least, he should have justified his action to other team members. A little transparency would have helped. But he did not care and thus he was unable to manage his image. Finally he had to face the King.

Perceptions are formed quickly, but changing perceptions takes a long, long time and is a huge task. It is better not to take a chance. You should be in control, and should manage your own brand and image. And you should begin now.

Work as a team

Coming together is a beginning. Keeping together is progress. Working together is success.—Henry Ford

Once upon a time, there was a young man who worked as an office boy in a factory. He was assigned to the finance department.

One day, the King, the head of the factory, was on a round. It was late in the night when he saw this young man moving around. He was surprised because all support staff were supposed to leave the factory by 6 p.m. He asked him, 'My son, why are you still here?'

The young man replied confidently 'Your highness, I'm waiting to serve the next round of tea to these people in finance. You know they have been working late for the last few days to complete the month-end report.'

'But your duty ends at 6 p.m., no?' asked the King.

'The finance department works late for the first few days every month. I stay back with them. They need to have tea and coffee to stay fresh.'

'But who has asked you to stay back?'

'No one, your highness.'

'Then why are you still here?' asked the King.

'I think it is my duty to serve them, your highness.'

'Do you get paid extra for it?'

'No, your highness.' The young man explained, 'Your highness, a few months ago, I heard from my colleague that the finance department made a big mistake in the month-end report. Then, I heard the finance folk talking about how tiring it was to work late nights. They also complained about not getting any refreshments late in the night. I understood that they requested the administration department as well, which was refused as that would be of additional cost to the company. I thought about it and decided to work late for a few days every month.'

The young man paused and added, 'Your highness, after all we work for the same company. If a little effort from me helps the team, why shouldn't I make it?'

The King was amazed at the thought process of that uneducated young man. He said, 'In my career, I have never come across such a silent team worker. This is amazing. Even the finance team does not know how much you contribute to their, and the company's, success.'

The young man's face shone with pride. He smiled shyly.

The King said, 'People fight for individual success but they should understand that it has no meaning if they fail as a team. You will certainly be rewarded.'

The King patted his back, which was the greatest reward for the young man. He lived happily ever after.

This is one of the most difficult issues we face as we join the corporate world. The issue is about changing our focus from individual success to collective success. In the corporate world, we win together, we lose together. No point in scoring a century to score a record, when the team loses the game because you played too cautiously to score your own century. If the team is successful, we are successful. In the corporate world, we cannot achieve anything individually.

Learning the trick to work in a team is the way forward.

Teamwork is all about sharing a common goal, moving ahead by trusting each other, learning from each other, and thus winning together. However, this is easier said than done. It requires immense mental strength and ability to talk to ourselves, forcing ourselves to change. We need to be flexible to adapt to the need of the team.

And it is so easy to break a team. It happens when 'I' comes before 'we'. It's a natural human trait as we love our success the most, and, at times, feel that we can conquer the world alone. That is when the team starts to fail. We should believe in the team because we want to be with the team, not because we were 'asked' to be with the team. We genuinely need to be part of it.

Every member in a team will be different—from a different culture, different background, or different organizational hierarchy. We need to understand them and appreciate their viewpoints. We must appreciate that each has something unique to contribute, which is why they are in the team.

Every member also has expectations from the other members; we need to talk about them, communicate all the time. There may be friction as we move along; it is for us to resolve the issue and still stay positive. Let us learn to give up individual egos and work towards common goals. Appreciation, gratitude and empathy are the things that keep a team going. Ultimately, isn't it fun to celebrate with friends than be alone? Let us start enjoying the power of togetherness, which is truly amazing. The people who learn this early will definitely emerge as winners from this jungle.

Manage conflict

Honest disagreement is often a good sign of progress.
—Mahatma Gandhi

Once upon a time, there was a young lady who was in the product development department of a manufacturing company. She was an outsourced employee, not on the payroll. Her job was to follow up on project deadlines and report the progress to the marketing head.

One day, the King, the CEO, wanted a project review meeting. This young lady went around and met the project leaders and asked for the information. One leader refused to share any data, so she reported the matter to the marketing head, who in turn reported that to the King. The King was furious and called for a meeting involving the marketing head, the project manager, and the young lady.

The King asked the young lady, 'Why is this report incomplete?'

The young lady readily replied, 'Your highness, I tried my best but I could not get some information.'

The marketing head supported her, said, 'Your highness, this poor girl followed up almost every day. She even mentioned this meeting with you, but the project manager refused to share the information.'

The King turned to the project manager and demanded an explanation. He replied, 'Even if she follows up every moment, I will never be comfortable to share this data with her.'

'You have no right to keep company data to yourself,' replied the marketing head.

'I have, and I will explain why. First, let me ask you this: if this data were so critical, why didn't you call me yourself?'

'That is not my job. I have enough on my plate. I can't waste my time on unnecessary follow-ups.'

The discussion quickly turned into a fight and the King had to intervene. He asked the young lady to leave the meeting, and asked the project manager, 'Do you have the data ready with you?'

'Yes, I have it with me to share with you,' the project manager replied calmly.

'Then, why you did not share it with the young lady?'

'Your highness, this is confidential data. As per company policy, I am not supposed to share such information with outsiders. This young lady is not our employee, therefore I decided against it. I tried to reach the marketing manager, even sent him a couple of mails, but he seemed too busy to reply. I also sent a message through the young lady for him to call me back, but unfortunately he didn't.'

The King looked at the marketing manager and said, 'You should have responded!'

The marketing manager felt ashamed and realized his mistake. He apologized to the project manager. And they lived happily ever after.

Everybody wants to be winner in this corporate jungle. Everybody is looking for 'that' power and 'that' success at a pace no one else has achieved. But you must accept that you are not the only ones gunning for success, fame or recognition. You have others around you. Success being relative and the top of the ladder being narrow, corporate life will never be free of conflict. You need to learn how to carefully steer through conflict situations.

Quite often, you assume things and first jump to conclusions about certain people or issues and then react later. You do not ask. You do not try to understand the other's mind. You take positions and make it even worse by taking others' reactions personally. You force a professional matter to become a personal matter. Often, you hear about a person and draw an inference about his or her intentions. Such a preconceived mindset often pushes you into conflicts.

At times, you choose not to give up, even when you realize that you are wrong. Or it can be the other way round—when another person behaves in the same way, and you are not able to make them admit that they are wrong. These situations lead to endless arguments, loss of respect, exchanges of foul words and general ill will. Sometimes, the situation becomes so much worse that finding a middle ground becomes almost impossible.

Emotion plays a major role in conflicts. Let us look at the rationale behind a comment or an action before arriving at a decision in our minds. There is nothing wrong in arguing, but there is a thin line between arguing and taking a position to defend a viewpoint. You need to be aware of this line. You must listen to each other, appreciate each other's viewpoints, show respect to others and tweak your opinions if required. You should not close your minds, you should be open and understanding.

In the story, the marketing manager had a preconceived notion about the project manager, and he was not ready to change this opinion. That is why the conflict started. If the King hadn't intervened with an open mind, the two managers would have taken the conflict to an unproductive level.

You need to collaborate with each other. You should be professional, rational and emotion-free. If a problem can be solved by discussing and sharing knowledge, why pick a fight? Discussions will then be productive and healthy. Inability to manage conflict can be the biggest deterrent to your way to the top. It will affect individual as well as team performance. If your current way of dealing with a problem leads to conflict, you must learn a new way to act. You must do that as soon as you can.

Plan and execute

A good plan, violently executed now, is better than a perfect plan next week.—George S. Patton

Once upon a time, the King, the marketing head of a company, was launching new products in the market. After many years, the company had decided to refresh the entire product range. It was an important time for everybody in the organization, and the King himself took utmost interest in it.

The King reviewed the strategy carefully; he knew that he

could not take any chances. He told his team, 'The products have to be different, the concepts have to be new. We should take the consumers as well as the competitors by surprise.'

Every week, he went through the plan carefully to ensure that it was flawless.

Since the company dealt with seasonal products, nearly 70 per cent of its sales took place during the summer (April to June). It would take at least six months to develop these products after the final plan was approved. The King was busy making the perfect plan without realizing that time was running out for an April launch.

In a planning meeting in October, the King was reviewing the status of the latest designs. He was still not happy with them. He suggested more changes. The team agreed to put the changed design up for a review the next week. But then a young man from sales said, 'Your highness, I urge you to finalize the design today.'

'But, young man, the team is not ready as yet!'

'I need the products in the market in April. There is no point in launching these new products after the season is over. We would only have wasted money, time, energy and effort. The only result of such a delayed launch will be an unsold inventory!'

'I understand, but I need to have the final plan to give a go-ahead.'

'Your highness, what is the point of a perfect plan if it cannot be executed on time? You know that we need six months to develop the products after we finalize the plan. You also know that we have only three months to sell our products. I sincerely urge you to approve the plans now!'

The King thought for a while and said, 'Thank you for getting me out of my musing. I was so obsessed with perfect planning that I almost forgot that we also need to execute it!'

Even the King learnt a lesson that day.

The team worked overnight and the plan was finalized by next morning. The King rewarded the young man for saying the obvious, which everybody understood but no one articulated. And they lived happily ever after.

We humans are gifted with too much intelligence. Thus most of our plans are great, but we fail to execute them. An effective plan is imperative. If one fails to plan, then he plans to fail! But that should be just the starting point. The onus is on us to execute our plan as well.

When we take up an assignment, we seldom try to understand its objective. We seldom ask 'why' and 'when'. Thus, at times, we go ahead without proper perspective, which becomes a hindrance to our progress. We need to clarify the purpose, so that we can plan in the right direction and make achievable plans. An understanding of the final requirement will enable us to break down the task by elements and lay down an action plan that can be better executed. Let us review the plan at every required interval and tweak it to suit the latest needs or any changes.

Strategy and planning may be heavy words but let us not sit back and think that they are meant for the top management alone. Every day, everybody at every level is required to draw up a plan and then execute it. From the first day in this corporate world, we need to know how to balance planning and execution. Let us own an idea and then execute it. Never undervalue execution vis-à-vis strategization. Both are equally important for you to succeed. The truth is that we can have the best ideas but if we don't know how to implement them, we will not be needed in the corporate world. We will be successful when we have great ideas but focus equally to ensure that the ideas are executed well. A balanced approach is preferred. We must apply this learning from the day we hit the corporate world.

Attain alignment

Harmony exists in difference no less than in likeness, if only the same keynote governs both parts.—Margaret Fuller

Once upon a time, there was a young man who was the deputy to the marketing head of a company. He had a mind of his own and always behaved in a way far more mature than his years. The King, the CEO, loved him for his brilliance.

When the marketing head quit, the King decided not to recruit any new incumbent. He wanted to try his luck with this young man and handed over to him the major responsibility of heading the marketing function. Many of his peers did not like this move but this young man wasn't bothered, as he was confident about delivering what was expected of him. The fact that the King had entrusted him with such a big responsibility boosted his confidence.

The marketing department planned some new product launches under the leadership of this young man. The team worked hard to deliver the new range and the ad campaign supporting it. The products were launched but, surprisingly, the market response was extremely poor. The young man was shocked. He travelled the market extensively and realized that the consumers and the dealers liked the product. Yet, nothing moved and sales went down by the month!

The King was frustrated with the result, having spending enormous money on product development and advertising campaigns. He conducted review meetings but did not get any satisfactory answer. He then decided to travel the market to understand the real issue. On his return to the office, he called the young man and said, 'I am upset with your approach.'

The young man looked surprised, as the King continued, 'I did warn you, but you never bothered to listen to me. I told you earlier that we were losing market share every month. You didn't agree. Now, after scrutinizing the market, I am convinced. What is your justification, young man?'

The young man felt challenged, for he had no answer to offer. He looked at the King helplessly and said, 'You know we have launched new products. I thought I could use that to salvage the situation. The products are great and we did everything possible to support them in the market. Yet the sales are not picking up. Tell me, your highness, where did I go wrong?'

'If you wish to know the truth, here it is. You never took the pains to align your thoughts and ideas with the other members in the organization. You wanted to go all alone with your strategy. This is where you went wrong. Often, I advised you that individual brilliance does not help an organization succeed. You need to move together as an organization. You need everyone's support to achieve your goal. People need to participate in the journey. You did not listen to me. You failed to explain to others why they should be party to your dream. You designed some great products, but your marketing strategy was never aligned to that of the frontline sales team. You tried to push through ideas that you believed were right; unfortunately, the others couldn't see the value in that! You can't force others to act your way. They need to understand your thinking. You failed to bring your vision alive, to translate it into action. You didn't include others when you devised your strategy. You didn't bother to explain the benefits to them. That is where you failed.'

'I am sorry, your highness. Please help me manage the crisis.'

'I will help you, young man, but make sure you learn from this experience.'

The King called for a meeting the next day with all the stakeholders and advised the young man to present the strategy for a re-launch of the products. All the leaders debated their ideas but finally agreed to a unified approach. The entire company thus went ahead with one vision in mind. There was no individual strategy, only one purpose and the collective zeal to win. The young man learnt his lesson and lived happily ever after.

People, people and people—that is what a corporate is made of. Not even for a moment can we ignore the fact that we are among people. Not aligning them on a task or on a need will be a sure recipe for failure. We will never be successful if we fail at aligning people to our vision.

It is not easy. Though we all work for a common goal, everybody in an organization is different and has his or her own agenda, priorities, biases, and opinions. Hence, everything that we want to do or propose may not be acceptable to all the others all the time. Aligning people is never an easy job but we have no option but to master this act.

Back in college, alignment was not so important. In fact, it was actually not needed most of the time. In student life, individual performance mattered; alignment with friends or teachers helped us lead nice campus lives, but, eventually, we had to attempt our examination on our own. In the corporate world, however, it is all about shared vision and shared performance. Each element of the system needs to perform individually to win as a team. People need to understand why we want certain things to be done, and what is there for them in it. Aligning visions before moving ahead with an idea will help us engage others in the task we are pursuing. It is an essential element at every stage of the corporate life. We should learn this at the beginning of our careers.

Think differently

Man often becomes what he believes himself to be. If I keep on saying to myself that I cannot do a certain thing, it is possible that I may end by really becoming incapable of doing it. On the contrary, if I have the belief that I can do it, I shall surely acquire the capacity to do it even if I may not have it at the beginning.—Mahatma Gandhi

Once upon a time, there was a Queen, who headed the HR department of a large multinational. The great recession had just passed by, but, interestingly, people in the company never felt the heat of such a great global economic phenomenon. Despite the recession, the company's performance was at an all-time high. People within the company, and outside, wondered. Some people called it a fluke, some called it luck. But most of them were clueless about how such great the results were achieved.

Late one evening, the Queen noticed a young man working quietly at his desk. She asked, 'What are you doing in office so late, young man?' The young man was engrossed in her job and couldn't hear her. The Queen tapped his back and asked again.

The young man looked up and replied, 'I'm making a short film.'

'A film?' The Queen was surprised.

'Yes, your highness. I just found out how we performed so well when everyone faced challenges last year. Like the others, I too had expected our economy-driven industry to be in peril. Then I realized that we, as a team, are different.'

'But why are you wasting your time? That is not your job,' said the Queen.

The young man smiled and said, 'I had some spare time and thus thought of spending it this way. When I look at the last few months, I notice that our performance is not phenomenal by chance—we took many good decisions as well as many contrarian views, and all that helped.'

The Queen wondered for a while and said, 'But then how does it matter now? The past is past.'

'It matters, your highness. It shows me the strength of our leadership. It tells me that we have the right leaders steering the company. It reassures me that I haven't erred in joining this company.'

'What will you do with this film?'

'I want to show this to all employees and tell them the story. All employees should understand the facts behind this outstanding result. They will feel proud and it will enhance our employee commitment.'

The Queen said, 'I am amazed! I wonder how such a young man like you can think beyond your own space and do wonders. Please show me your work whenever you finish.'

A few days later, the young man showed her the film. She was enthralled by his ability to put the story together. She said thoughtfully, 'I was thinking how we miss out on talent. I was lucky to walk past you the other day, or else, your entire effort may have gone down the drain. Let us quickly meet the CEO and show him your work;

it deserves much more applause.'

The young man showed his work to the King, who was amazed. Thrilled with joy, he said, 'I wish I have more young men like you in this company.' The King ordered the film to be shared with all employees and partners. The young man was rewarded. And he lived happily ever after.

Have you ever wondered why no one appreciates you for drawing a cartoon of your boss in our office diary? At a meeting, why can't you play a song to lighten the atmosphere? Why can't you get up and tell people to call off a meeting when it is not making sense?

It's all because a corporate is run by rules, which no one is supposed to breach. But while that is all fine, it does not mean that you can't think differently. It does not mean that you can't challenge yourselves. Some call them out-of-the-box thinkers, some call them geniuses, some call them madmen, some call them intellectuals, but everyone appreciates such professionals.

We humans are creative by nature. As you grew up, you were flooded with new ideas. You wondered all the time and your imaginations were unstoppable. Somehow, with the passage of time, you tend to become less creative. Why should that be? Why should you kill the thinker in you? Your creative mind should not die or fade away over time.

Life should not change once you join the corporate world; the only change should be that you must adjust to certain routines and rules which are a part of life in every corporate. In this new life, even as you diligently perform the daily chores, your creative thinking should not take a backseat. Some people can be imaginative and creative even when they are hard-pressed to deliver to deadlines, always running against time. Everybody respects such people, who can retain their difference while performing even the most routine activities.

Apart from thinking differently, you also need to gear yourselves to think ahead. Why should your bosses do all the strategizing while you execute what they think? What stops you from thinking at the level of your boss, or even ahead of him? You are new to this world, and your mind is still uncluttered. You are intelligent people; you must stimulate your brain constantly and challenge yourselves to get ready for the next level.

This ability to think differently is a catalyst. It can make the difference between a normal career progression and a fast–track career. It would be a rare senior who would not want his junior to think ahead of his level. But in reality, most of us fail to wear our thinking caps once we start our daily chores in the corporate world. If some people hate you for being different, let that not bother you. They are probably just insecure. Your imaginations should not be pulled down into the mire of ordinariness by such people. Let yourself marvel again, like you did years ago. Start that journey now.

Watch your back

You never really know your friends from your enemies until the ice breaks.—Eskimo proverb

Once upon a time, there was a young man who joined the corporate world. As a finance professional, he was a little different than the typical accountant who worried about numbers all the time. The young man had a knack for business and always looked for solutions that supported the business. Soon, he was appreciated by everybody for his practical approach and his ability to provide solutions. He became popular among his seniors and peers.

The company had a system of recognizing good talents and putting them into fast-track careers. Only one per cent of the employees were selected for the accelerated career path. This young man became one, purely through merit. Being a top talent, he got a promotion within a year of joining the company. He was happy to get recognized for his efforts, and worked even more diligently and intelligently for the company. The King, the CEO of the company, was pleased with his performance and planned to promote him again the following year. In fact, in a meeting, the King informally committed another promotion to the young man. Soon, he would reach a level where no one at his age had been.

The young man was simple at heart; his whole world was centred around the company. He was always busy with his work. He never realized that many of his colleagues did not like his success and were poisoning the King's mind against him.

Through the office grapevine, a senior officer in the purchase department heard about the King's commitment. He hated the news. He didn't like the fact that this young man would soon hold a post as high as his own, without the years of experience. He hatched a plan to work on the King's mind. At every opportunity, this senior office subtly dropped negative points about the young man to the King. He ensured that the King got the impression that the reputation of this young man was inflated and he was not mature enough to handle any further responsibility. In fact, it was slowly established that this young man is not fit to be a top talent.

The doubt slowly took seed in the King's mind; he started rethinking his own decision about promoting this young man too quickly. Yet, somehow, he was not convinced that his assessment could have been so wrong. He wanted to reassess his own views. He started meeting this young man more frequently. Interestingly, at every meeting, the King was reassured that his positive impression about of the young man was correct. The King wanted to get to the truth. He thought a lot and found a common thread. He realized that the senior officer never criticized the young man when the latter was present. So, the young man never got an opportunity to defend himself. The King understood the game and decided to give the young man a fair chance.

Thereafter, whenever the senior officer spoke ill of the young man, the King immediately called the young man in for an explanation. Not surprisingly, every time, the young man proved the senior officer to be wrong. The officer realized that his trick was revealed, and, within a few months, he left the company. That day, the King called the young man and said, 'Here is your promotion letter, young man. You are doing really well and we are all proud to have you here.'

The young man smiled and said, 'Thank you, your highness. I know you saved me this time.'

The King said, 'But you need to save yourself, my young friend. In this journey, you will meet many people who would like to pull down a talent like you. Be careful!' The young man nodded. He had received an important lesson and lived happily ever after.

The corporate world is not a bed of roses. Obstacles will be part of this life. Overcoming the hurdles is the way to success. It is natural that many people will not want you to succeed. The psychology is simple—they feel that your success will hamper their career advancement. And so, competition will creep in the moment you step into this new world. Healthy competition is always welcome—it challenges us to deliver better results—but when the competition turns ugly and people deliberately play against you to hinder your growth, you need to be careful and protect your back.

When you enter a team, there will be a set of people who welcome you and help you to settle in quickly. There is also a great possibility that all of them may not be so cooperative. It is natural to find some people who will not be too happy with your inclusion in the team, and hence will try and play spoilsport. The idea is to identify them quickly and work to ensure that they do not create any trouble for you.

It may be possible that you are promoted earlier than your batchmates. It may also happen that you are asked to supervise colleagues who were once your peers. Do you think it will be easy for those people to accept you as a boss? Would you like to be in a similar situation? Think about yourself. Won't you get hurt if a similar situation cropped up for you as well? You need to learn how to manage such situations. You need to allow people to take their time to accept you. Trying to embed too many changes in no time can jeopardize your effort. Allow reasonable time and space to others so that the very idea that you are now senior to them sinks in. Talk to them straight, be fair and nice to each individual and avoid any favouritism. The sooner you establish the new working relationship, the better will it be that for you and the others.

At times, ego or a personal problem can work against you. It isn't easy to please everybody on the corporate journey. In fact, you are not here to please everybody; you are here to work for a company. Work-related issues may lead to friction and arguments and conflicts. In that battle, someone has to lose. Though a win–win situation is desirable, it may not always be the outcome. This too may lead your colleagues to work against you.

You must be careful. You must watch your backs as well. Anticipate blows from your peers, seniors, juniors, even outsiders. When you see the blow coming, it is easy to tackle. But if the enemy works against you, behind your back, you need to learn the trick to keep a guard. The sooner we master this art, the faster will be our progress in the jungle.

Take care of yourself

No one saves us but ourselves. No one can and no one may. We ourselves must walk the path.—The Buddha

Once upon a time, there lived a King who was the CEO of a large corporation. People called him Wonderman. At the age of fifty years, he looked no more than thirty-five. An active sportsperson, he was fit like a college student. He was always energetic and agile. No one ever saw him tense, even when his business faced crises. His positive energy and smile were infectious.

One day, a young man joined the company. He held an MBA from a premier management institute. He was intelligent and hardworking. He had joined the corporate world to make a mark and so he worked almost fifteen hours a day, always delivering better results than expected. Soon, he became the blue-eyed boy of the Minister, his boss.

After many days, the Minister came to the King and said, 'Your Highness, I think I made a mistake. I backed the wrong horse and made a blunder by promoting this young man too early. He is not as good as I had expected. His performance has gone down significantly over the last few months. He makes mistakes frequently. I cannot bank on him any more.'

The King smiled and said, 'Don't worry, Minister, all will be fine. Can I meet him tomorrow?'

The young man was sent to the palace. The King met him in the courtyard and asked, 'Young man, what is wrong with you these days?'

The young man looked astounded.

The King went on, 'Have you looked at yourself? Have you seen the change in yourself in the last two years? I remember meeting you earlier; you were a bundle of energy. Don't you see that you have burnt yourself up completely?' After a pause, the King added, 'My friend, you are a human being, not a machine. Like your body, your brain requires rest too. How can you expect them to support you continuously?'

The young man agreed and said, 'I know, your highness. I feel tired these days. I can realize that I am not as sharp and intelligent as I was a few years ago.'

'No, you are the same. You still have all the potential to reach the top, but you need to change. Take a break and alter the course of your life. I was very clear from the day I joined the corporate world that I would give 101 per cent to this world, but I would also give 101 per cent to my own world.'

'What do you mean, your highness?' asked the young man.

'I can tell you what I do. I divide my day into three zones—body, mind, soul. I dedicate a few hours in the morning to my body. As I exercise, I get time with myself. That gives me an opportunity to think as well and plan for the day. I dedicate the day to my mind, through my work. And, in the evening, I dedicate time to my soul. I do what I want to do. I read, write, listen to music, watch a film or just spend time with family and friends.'

The young man said, 'But how do you manage your work within this short time? You hold such a responsible position!'

'I work backwards. I know the tasks in hand, and that helps me to prioritize my work. It helps me plan my day better. There is no right formula for it, but my own formula helps me.

'I have another piece of advice for you. You must learn to celebrate. Remember, you will not get a raise or a promotion every day. But then, you need to find a reason that will get you going. You need to look for reasons to celebrate. Every time I felt that I have achieved something or contributed to my company's success, I celebrated. Sometimes I celebrated with my colleagues, sometimes with friends and family. Sometimes I was alone, but I celebrated. All celebrations may not be lavish, it can even be just a cup of tea, but you need to seize that moment. This funny habit of mine got me going, as I looked for the next day to celebrate again.'

The young man nodded as the King smiled and said, 'So go ahead and conquer the world. You have bright prospects. Please don't spoil your life by working late every day and eating pizza late in the night, every night!'

As the young man left the palace, he knew that he would live happily ever after.

There is a lovely term called 'work–life balance', the meaning of which some of us don't understand and the rest of us don't want to understand. I suppose it is one of those things that are good to talk about but difficult to implement.

Each one of us thinks that he is the most indispensable person in the organization and that life would come to a standstill without him. I agree that we need to be responsible, and that our success depends on the results we deliver each time, every time. However, we must always define our day between 'work' and 'life'. There is a thin line between these two. Does this mean that there is no life in work? No way. If one feels so at any point, that would be the end of his corporate success. We must love the corporate life but must also know how to take care of ourselves.

Who are you fooling by working late every day, then ordering a pizza and a soft drink when you suddenly realize that you need to eat to survive, and then continuing with your work till midnight? Who are you fooling when you take out your computer every weekend to complete that urgent assignment, which you could not finish by Friday evening in office? Who are you fooling when you get up at 8.30 a.m on a Monday, still tired, and rush to the office with your head completely blocked? Who are you fooling when you slowly give up your favourite outdoor sports to settle down next to your laptop?

Take a step back and think about yourself. I agree that you need to give more than desired to this corporate world, but you must realize that you also have a life beyond that. You have a responsibility towards your body, your mind, your soul. You must keep them happy as well. Lost time and age will never come back. Many successful people later regret not taking care of themselves at the right age.

You need to have an agile mind all the time; a tired mind will not be able to take care of either you or the company you work for. And remember, no one will do this job for you—you need to take care of yourself.

There is no right formula; it will be different everyday. Each stage of your life will demand a little extra from you, and you must strike the balance. Don't try to rush through life all the time. Learn to celebrate. You are in a journey of many years; you need to be fresh and nimble till the end. Sit back, relax and enjoy your corporate journey. Success will follow you.

***

Mr Chatterjee looked at us. We knew it was the end of his last session. There was complete silence. I was the first to stand up, and, without realizing I started clapping. Everyone followed suit. The sound of applause grew louder and louder. I don't know how long we all clapped. Then Mr Chatterjee intervened, 'Thank you folks. I am honoured. But before I ask the big question, let us summarize what we learnt in the day. Who will take the lead?'

One of the participants said, 'I am now confident that I will emerge as a winner from this corporate jungle.'

Mr Chatterjee said, 'These are the lessons that I have learnt from life over many years. I am happy that I could share them with you.'

The participant said, 'We learnt the power of networking, both the good and the bad. We also learnt how to be prepared and be present—present mentally.'

Another participant added, 'I think I learnt the power of taking calculated risks. I also learnt that I should not confine myself to my predefined job but think out of box and do that extra bit, which is unstated.'

I said, 'I know the value of the team goal and team success. I now know that individual success will always follow if we are successful as a team. These sessions also taught me the importance of walking together after aligning a goal. It will help me manage conflicts too.'

'And, not to forget, we learnt about being aware of the people who would like to pull us down,' piped up another.

'Learn to celebrate, make yourself happy. Always remember to take care of yourself. You can't delegate that. No one will do that for you. If you do not exist in the right shape and form, both physically and mentally, success will never follow you,' said Mr Chatterjee.

It was time to end the last session. Mr Chatterjee looked at me and said, 'Now is the time for the big question.'

I was curious and waited for Mr Chatterjee to speak.

He said, 'The big question is—do we need any more sessions?'

I smiled and said, 'No sir. I am happy that I challenged you, or we would have never got the treasure of our life.'

Mr Chatterjee smiled and said, 'Let's huddle together once before we go back to our journeys.'

We all locked shoulders in a huddle, feeling the warmth in each other. I felt confident that I could begin my journey to emerge as a winner from this corporate world.

ACKNOWLEDGEMENTS

Many people, knowingly and unknowingly, contributed as I wrote this book:

My readers, for their encouragement through numerous emails, FB, LinkedIn and personal messages.

My corporate colleagues over the years. Many of them would probably never realize how they have contributed to this book. But a lot of the invaluable knowledge I have learnt from them has found its way into this book.

Many corporate aspirants, whom I meet in various colleges, forums and who have time and again told me the need for a book that can help them navigate their way to a successful career.

Vaishali Mathur, senior commissioning editor, Penguin India, for having the patience of reading the manuscript and accepting it. I still remember the call from her when she said, 'I have really liked the work.'

Udayan Mitra, publisher, Allen Lane and Portfolio, for accepting the work under Portfolio. His positive attitude and encouragement has made me believe again that 'the corporate world needs this book'. Without Udayan's guidance this book would not have taken the shape that it has today.

Ambar Sahil Chatterjee and Monidipa Mondal, for

their splendid editing. I am very lucky to have had them as my editors.

My family and friends, for being with me throughout this journey and giving me constant encouragement.

Little Rayan and Anavi, for helping me to find the 'right' quotations.

And Sayanti, for her encouragement, love and support.